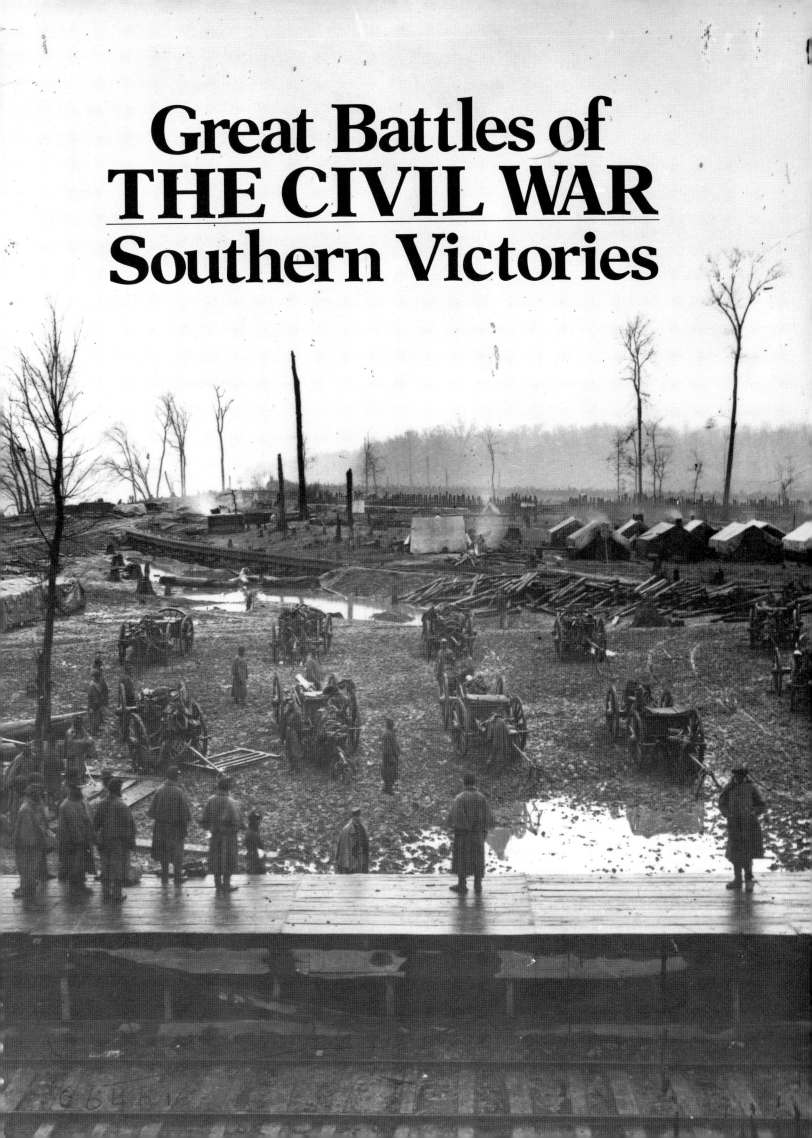

# Great Battles of
# THE CIVIL WAR
# Southern Victories

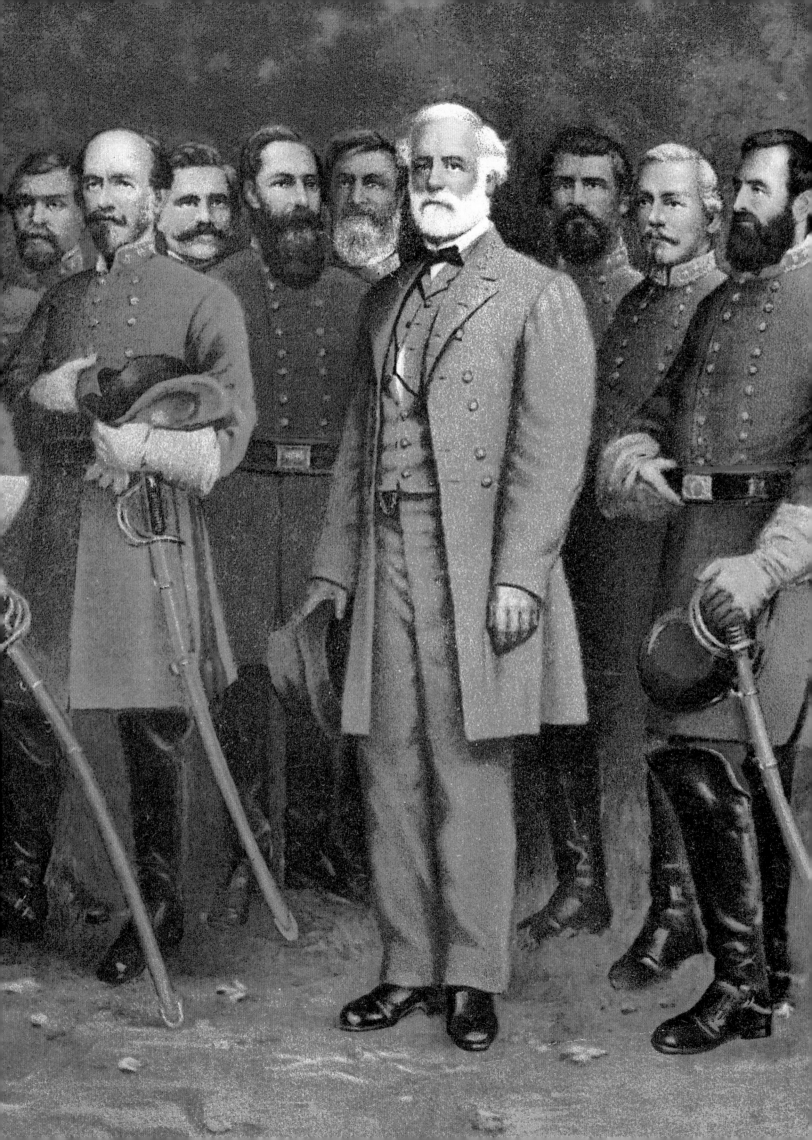

# Great Battles of
# THE CIVIL WAR
# Southern Victories

## Swafford Johnson

**Brompton**

First published in 1992 by
Brompton Books Corporation
15 Sherwood Place
Greenwich, CT 06830 USA

ISBN 1-890221-00-7

Printed in China

Reprinted in 1997

**Page 1:** *A Tennessee artillery battery.*

**Page 2:** *Robert E Lee and his generals.*

**Pages 4-5:** *Uniforms and insignia of the CSA Army.*

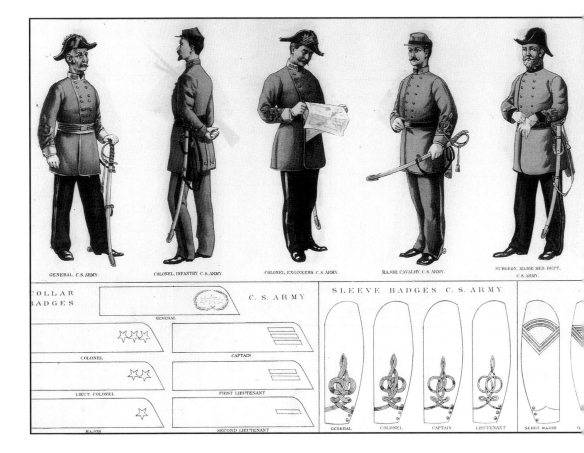

# CONTENTS

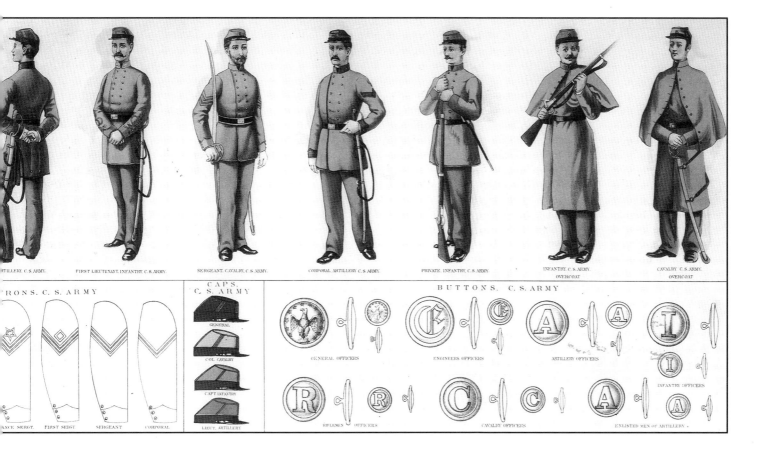

# THE OPENING GUNS

**O**n 20 December 1860, a convention of delegates meeting in Charleston, South Carolina, unanimously voted to pass this ordinance.

We, the people of the State of South Carolina, in Convention assembled, do declare and ordain, and it is hereby declared and ordained, that the ordinance adopted by us in Convention, on the 23rd day of May, in the year of our Lord 1788, whereby the Constitution of the United States of America was ratified, and also all Acts and parts of Acts of the General Assembly of this State ratifying the amendments of the said Constitution, are hereby repealed, and that the union now subsiding between South Carolina and other States under the name of the United States of America is hereby dissolved.

It happened at last, the thing long predicted and long feared: the United States, which had fought so fiercely for nationhood and felt themselves to be the hope of the world, were beginning to fall apart. A state had seceded from the Union. Others were ready to follow its lead.

The issues swirling around slavery had, beginning from the inception of the country, tended increasingly to split the nation along sectional lines. Among other corollary issues were the contending doctrines of federalism and of states' rights. Federalism, strongest in the North, proclaimed the primacy of the federal government and its laws; while states' rights doctrine, strongest in the South, upheld the primacy of each state's government and the states' right to nullify Federal laws they did not like – and, in extremity, to sever their bonds with the Union entirely.

Thus over the years two sections of the country pulled apart in economy (the North was more industrialized), in temperament and in culture. On both sides, fear and suspicion gradually supplanted goodwill and reason. Eventually the situation had grown out of control of even the wisest of men. The divisiveness came to a head with the election of Abraham Lincoln, whom the South perceived as a rabid abolitionist. In reality, Lincoln was comparatively a moderate on the issue. He regarded slavery as a great evil, writing at one point, "If slavery is not wrong, then nothing is wrong." But

**Below:** *An early cotton gin. It made cotton the staple crop of the South, increasing the demand for slaves.*

**Opposite:** *Jefferson Davis, US senator and former cabinet officer, became president of the CSA.*

Lincoln was willing to go to any lengths to resolve tensions peacefully; if that meant tolerating slavery for the time being, he would tolerate it.

By the time of Lincoln's inauguration, on 4 March 1861, he was faced with a rival government of seven Southern states calling themselves the Confederate States of America: South Carolina, Mississippi, Florida, Alabama, Georgia, Louisiana, and Texas. Following the lead of South Carolina, these states had responded to Lincoln's election by seceding from the Union, had drawn up a constitution, appointed a president, and claimed all Federal property within their borders.

Lincoln's opposite, Confederate President Jefferson Davis, was already occupying his office and planning how best to take over Union garrisons in the South. There were three of these in Florida, far from the centers of government; it was on the fourth garrison that the attention of the whole country came to rest – Fort Sumter, in Charleston Harbor.

The importance and the vulnerability of Fort Sumter had become clear even before Lincoln or Davis had taken office. After South Carolina seceded, state authorities sent a commission to President James Buchanan to arrange for transfer of Federal property to the Confederacy. Buchanan, who was not entirely unsympathetic to the South, met the commissioners unofficially and told them he would not change the status quo in Charleston Harbor. But soon after this the status quo did change ominously. Acting on his own, Major Robert Anderson, Federal commander in the harbor, loaded his men on boats and took them from the old Revolutionary Fort Moultrie, near the mainland, to the more defensible Fort Sumter, an unfinished pentagonal brick edifice three miles out in the harbor. The significance of Anderson's move was

**Above:** *Major Anderson left Fort Moultrie on Christmas night 1860. The troops moved to Fort Sumter.*

**Opposite:** *A Currier & Ives print of the attack on Fort Sumter in Charleston Harbor, 12 April 1861.*

not lost on Confederate authorities. In January President Buchanan sent a boat of provisions to the fort, which was low on both food and munitions; the boat was fired on from the South Carolina mainland and turned back. The state government decreed that no supplies of any kind were to be allowed in. By the time Lincoln took office Fort Sumter was isolated and running out of food.

The president decided neither to abandon the fort nor to initiate hostilities, but rather to send a boatload of provisions to the garrison. In notifying the governor of South Carolina of that action Lincoln was in effect challenging the Confederates to respond: if hostilities were to begin, it must be the South's doing. The next day, 7 April, the response came: General Pierre G T Beauregard, Confederate commander in Charleston, cut off communications between Charleston and the fort and began to organize Confederate forces in the harbor. On 11 April Beauregard sent a demand for evacuation to Major Anderson. Sumter's commander, realizing the terrible momentum that was gathering about his command, replied that he would evacuate on 15 April unless he was attacked or received further orders from Washington. Suspecting, correctly, that this would not satisfy the Confederate authorities, Anderson assured the aides who delivered the ultimatum, "Gentlemen, if you do not batter the fort to pieces about us, we shall be starved out in a few days."

The momentum of events rolled on, pulled by the seem-

ingly irresistible magnet of war. At 3:20 in the morning on 12 April the next note came to Major Anderson: We have the honor to notify you that [Beauregard] will open the fire . . . in one hour from this time." Greatly upset, Major Anderson accompanied the Confederate messengers back to their boat. Pressing their hands in farewell, he choked, "If we never meet in this world again, God grant that we may meet in the next." (Among Anderson's acquaintances on the other side was Beauregard, his artillery instructor at West Point.)

Surrounding Fort Sumter in a wide circle on the mainland and islands around the harbor, the guns of the Confederacy were aimed and ready. Learning of Anderson's final words, General Beauregard sent firing orders at about four in the morning to Captain George S James and the James Island battery. Captain James positioned his men. When they were ready he turned to his friend Roger A Pryor and said to him, "You are the only man to whom I would give up the honor of firing the first gun of the war." Shaken, Pryor declined. At 4:30 in the morning of 12 April 1861, Captain James pulled the firing lanyard of a ten-inch mortar, and the first shot of the war arched into the sky.

It was not until after daylight that Federal guns began responding from within the fort. The slow rate of return fire showed the Confederates that the Federals were low on ammunition and were mounting only token resistance. After three hours of steady firing there were no casualties to either side.

Three Federal warships appeared outside the harbor in midmorning. The defenders in the fort cheered and flag salutes were exchanged, but after a few hours the ships turned and sailed away. Federal firing ceased at dusk. All through the night the Confederate batteries kept up their pounding while the defenders anxiously tried to sleep. About dawn on 13 April the batteries of Fort Moultrie began pouring hot shot into the fort, and the effects were soon seen: the

**Above:** *Interior of Fort Sumter during the bombardment. The shelling produced no casualties but the defenders' position was plainly impossible.*

**Below:** *The Confederate commander of Charleston, P G T Beauregard, accepted the surrender of Fort Sumter on 13 April. The Union evacuated the next day.*

Union barracks, supposedly fireproof, were in flames. The weak Federal return fire slowed still further, to one shot every five minutes, as soldiers in the fort were detailed to fight the flames and try to keep them from spreading to the magazine. Shortly after noon, the flagstaff of the fort was shot away and quickly repaired. But soon the Stars and Stripes were hauled down and replaced by a white flag.

A detachment was sent by boat to offer aid to the fort. They arrived to find that they had been preceded by ex-Senator Wigfall of Texas, who had apparently rowed out on his own to demand surrender. Wigfall had appeared in front of one of the fort's gun embrasures, to the considerable surprise of the Federal gunners. They had finally pulled Wigfall in before he was killed by his own side's fire. The ensuing negotiations were confused, what with two separate Confederate delegations and Major Anderson's uncertainties and anxieties – he and his men were begrimed with smoke and cinders and near exhaustion. But the outcome was inescapable. The garrison had taken some 4000 shells in 34 hours of nearly continuous bombardment and the Federals had few shells left to fire in reply. Finally Anderson capitulated, saying he would evacuate Fort Sumter on 14 April. Beauregard generously agreed that the Federals could salute their flag with cannons before leaving. By that point there still had been no casualties on either side.

As an ironic fate would have it, men were nonetheless destined to fall as a result of this battle. As the Federals fired their salute to the flag on 14 April, some sparks from the smouldering fire in the fort set off a paper-wrapped cannon cartridge as it was being loaded. The explosion killed Private Daniel Hough and wounded five other soldiers, one of whom soon died. These were the first casualties of the Civil War.

The fighting seemed rather dashing and decorous at Fort Sumter; to the Southerners it seemed the realization of all their fantasies of how easy it would be to send the Yankees running. All over the South there was revelry, dancing in the streets, young men joining up in thousands, showing off their grand new uniforms and guns to their families. They dreamed of glory and immortality and the romantic excitement of battle.

But elsewhere in the South one woman of Virginia, living in sight of Washington, wrote eloquently of her fears and heartbreak:

> I heard distinctly the drums beating in Washington. As I looked at the Capitol in the distance, I could scarcely believe my senses. That Capitol of which I had always been so proud! Can it be possible that it is no longer *our* capitol? Must this Union, which I was taught to revere, be rent asunder?

**Right:** *The Confederate flag flew over Fort Sumter throughout the war, despite several major Federal assaults. Confederate troops finally abandoned the ruined fort on 17 February 1865 before the approach of Union General Sherman's army.*

# FIRST AND SECOND MANASSAS

**A**fter the fall of Fort Sumter war fever swept across the country – or rather, the two countries. President Lincoln called for 75,000 three-month volunteers to suppress the Southern rebellion. Four more states seceded – Virginia, Arkansas, Tennessee, and North Carolina. The border states – Delaware, Maryland, Kentucky, and Missouri – stayed shakily loyal to the Union, even though the latter three were slave states. Both sides expected a short war, to be won in one or two decisive battles. Certainly no one foresaw the four years of agony that were to come.

There were essential differences in the strategy and aims of the two sections. The more formidable task was the Union's – in order to conquer the South the North had physically to invade, occupy, and hold its entire territory. This involved unprecedented commitments of men and supplies. On the other hand, the Confederacy's strategy seemed to call

**Left:** *Robert E Lee during his tenure as Superintendent of the US Military Academy (1852-55). Offered command of all the Federal forces on 18 April 1861, Lee declined, having decided that he could not raise his hand against his home state of Virginia.*

**Opposite:** *The young army officer Thomas J Jackson would earn his nickname "Stonewall" at First Manassas, where his brigade stoutly defended its position on Henry House Hill.*

for the defensive. As Northern armies advanced into the South their supply lines would steadily become longer and more tenuous as their numbers shrank due to attrition and the necessity of guarding lines of communication. The South thus had the advantage of fighting on and for its own territory, and also had, theoretically at least, the advantage of *interior lines* (because an invading army must stretch around and contain its enemy, that enemy, being more compact, can shift its forces much faster to any point on the perimeter along interior lines of communications).

At the beginning of the war the South probably had at least as good a chance of winning its war as the American colonies had of winning theirs. Moreover, Jefferson Davis confidently expected Great Britain and France to come to the rescue of the Confederacy; the threat of losing Southern cotton, Davis said, would bring them to the Confederate cause. In this, as in many other things, Davis miscalculated seriously. Great Britain at the beginning of the war had enough surplus cotton to last two years, and after that time found other sources.

(However, a good deal of Southern trading with Great

Britain – cotton out, arms and supplies in – did go on during the war. The North imposed a blockade of Southern ports from the outset, but it did not become effective until later in the war. In the South, blockade-running developed into a fine maritime art.)

Nearly all the commanding generals on both sides were West Pointers; as the war went on, a number of untrained leaders of genius arose, among them Nathan Bedford Forrest. But since military tradition was stronger in the South, the Confederacy got more than its share of the best military minds of the time; at the beginning of the war the North had no one to compare to Robert E Lee, Jackson, the two Johnstons, and Beauregard. This superiority of Confederate generalship in the early part of the war was clear to all concerned in the two great battles fought on a little stream called the Bull Run, near Manassas, Virginia.

Having resigned his commission in the US Army – and in the process declining an offer to command all Union forces – Robert Edward Lee was made a general in the Confederate army and given overall command of operations in his beloved home state of Virginia. In June and July of 1861 Americans began killing one another: Union forces were defeated near Fort Monroe, Virginia, and Federal general George B McClellan secured the western countries of Virginia for the Union (this area was soon to achieve statehood). Lee sent 11,000 men under General Joseph E Johnston to Harpers Ferry, near the entrance to Virginia's Shenandoah Valley, and 22,000 under General Pierre G T Beauregard to Manassas Junction, some 25 miles southwest of Washington. Lincoln,

despite objection that Union forces were too green, ordered General Irvin McDowell to drive Beauregard away from the important Manassas rail junction. Most of McDowell's 30,600 men were three-month volunteers and militia; only 800 were regular army. In support of McDowell, General Robert Patterson was ordered to keep Johnston in the Shenandoah in order to prevent his reinforcing Beauregard.

On 16 July, McDowell began advancing from Washington toward what everyone seemed to know would be the first great convulsion of the war. Many felt it would be the last. Confidently, the Union soldiers shouted, "On to Richmond!" Accompanying the Federal army were swarms of reporters, Congressmen, ladies with parasols and picnic baskets, and assorted sightseers – all off to see the war as if it were a fireworks show.

Marching on the Warrenton Turnpike, McDowell's Federal army reached Centreville, near Manassas, Virginia, on 18 July. At that point Beauregard's forces were vulnerable, though McDowell had no idea of that fact. Since the Union forces had become highly disorganized during the march, McDowell did not try a fullscale offensive (if he had, it might well have been successful). Meanwhile, Beauregard had received thorough intelligence concerning Union dispositions from a network of spies in Washington. He asked General Johnston to bring his forces over from the Shenandoah, where Patterson proved unable to contest their departure. On the 18th McDowell did try a reconnaissance in force against Beauregard's right. After a brisk skirmish at Blackburn's Ford on the Bull Run, the Federals were sent running

**Right:** *Confederate and Union movements toward Manassas Junction on 18 and 19 July.*
**Right bottom:** *Troop positions on 21 July 1861.*

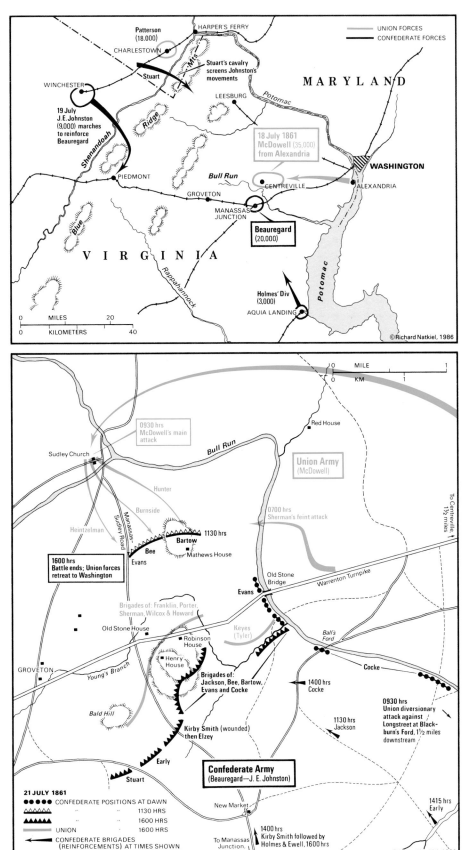

**Opposite:** *Confederate blockade-runners entering the harbor at St George, Bermuda. At first the Union blockade of the South was not very effective, but it became ever more so as the war progressed.*

back by the Confederates. The Southern commander in that skirmish was General James Longstreet, soon to be one of the great corps leaders of Robert E Lee's army. (In the South the affair at Blackburn's Ford is called the First Battle of Bull Run' to add to the confusion, the Northern names for the two large battles around the stream are the First and Second Bull Run).

McDowell's hesitation on the 28th allowed time for Johnston to move his 12,000 men east from the Shenandoah Valley. Most of that journey was made by railroad – the first major strategic troop movement by railroad in history. Among Johnston's generals was a strange, laconic brigade commander named Thomas J Jackson.

McDowell and Beauregard had been classmates at West Point and had studied the same tactics. Perhaps for that reason, they made identical plans for an offensive on 19 July: feint with the left, attack with the right. If both had been successful, the results could have been strange indeed – after brushing past each other like a swinging door, the Con-

**Left:** *Confederate troops moving by rail from the Shenandoah Valley to Manassas. Many new arrivals were marched directly from the railroad station to the battlefield.*

federates might have continued right into Washington and the Federals march into Richmond. But on the morning of the 19th, McDowell got his offensive underway first, and thereafter Beauregard and Johnston were on the defensive. McDowell made his feint on the Southern right, mounted a secondary attack on the enemy center, and took his right wing on a wide envelopment, marching the troops 15 miles through the broken and difficult landscape to attack the Rebel left flank.

Union general McDowell's plan was a perfectly good one, but it ran afoul of several problems. First, his troops were too inexperienced to execute with dispatch the intended wide envelopment of the Southern left flank. Second, Confederate observers on Signal Hill saw the movement and sent word to Beauregard: "Look out for your left; you are turned." Third, Beauregard had seen a cloud of dust on his left and realized the attack along the Warrenton Turnpike was a bluff to cover the move on his left. He began shifting divisions over to his left to oppose the oncoming Federals in the vicinity of Henry House Hill. As the Federals marched they could hear the whistles of the trains bringing Johnston's men to the battlefront. These arrivals were formed up on the railroad platform and marched directly into line.

Confident that every one of them could whip seven Yankees, the Confederate troops advanced from Henry House Hill towards the enemy. But then the Federals smashed into the Rebels, driving them back on to the hill. It seemed that the Federals were going to sweep the Rebels back down Henry House Hill. But defending that position was Thomas J Jackson and the brigade he had trained. He formed his men into a defensive nucleus on the hilltop. Seeing that stand, Confederate general Bernard E Bee entered history in his last moments of life. "Look at Jackson's Brigade," Bee shouted to his men, "It stands like a stone wall! Rally behind the Virginians!" And rally they did, stopping the advancing Federal troops in their tracks. And forever after, the general who led that stand would be called Stonewall Jackson, his men the Stonewall Brigade.

As Beauregard continued to strip his right and send men to the left, the Confederate line firmed up around Jackson on Henry House Hill. Finally Jackson led a counterattack on the Union right flank; sweeping around the hill in support rode the Rebel cavalrymen of young J E B ("Jeb") Stuart, another leader of that day destined for greatness. Jeb's men tore into a battalion of red-pantalooned New York Zouaves inflicting heavy casualties. At the most critical moment, just after two o'clock in the afternoon, on the Southern left, a Union artillery officer held his fire, mistaking blue-clad Rebel troops in his front for Federals; as a result, two powerful batteries fell into Southern hands and the Federals began to retreat. Now was Beauregard's great chance to pursue the enemy and annihilate them. However, at just that moment, Beauregard echoed the mistake of the Federal artillery commander: receiving a report that a large Federal force was moving on his supplies near Manassas, Beauregard pulled troops from his attack force to meet this threat. But the threat was a false alarm – it was Confederates marching towards the supplies, not Yankees. As Beauregard's advance slowed, dusk came on. The Confederacy had won the field that day of the first Manassas, but it was too late to pursue the enemy.

The Federals commenced an orderly retreat from the battlefield, moving up the Warrenton Turnpike. The Federal column, including numbers of civilian spectators who had not found the battle to be as much fun as they had expected, had to constrict to pass over a stone bridge over the Bull Run. Suddenly a Rebel battery dropped a few shells into the dense column near the bridge. There was an instant panic that quickly snowballed into a chaotic rout. By 22 July, Washington was inundated by the broken remains of its great army, which had become a mob of jaded, dirty, and demoralized men.

On the Confederate side there was a great and understandable jubilation over the triumph at Manassas. But the victory led to a dangerous overconfidence. Rebel soldiers had been confirmed in their illusion of invincibility.

Perhaps the South should have studied the casualty figures; they would have found the Union army had not been seriously damaged. Indeed, by the later standards of the war the First Manassas was not a particularly bloody contest – the South had 387 killed, 1582 wounded, 12 missing, for a total of 1981 casualties of the 32, 232 engaged; the Union suffered 418 killed, 1011 wounded, 1216 missing, for a total of 2645 casualties of 28,452 engaged. The contrast in the numbers of missing is notable; but the fact remained that the Union army was only marginally more hurt than the Confederate – and the North had virtually endless supplies of manpower, whereas the South was severely limited in that regard. The day after the First Manassas, a young Federal general named George B McClellan took command in Washington and from the shattered Union forces of the First Manassas began rebuilding the army.

As will be described in the next chapter, Stonewall Jackson went on to his Shenandoah Valley Campaign of summer 1862. During that operation, Jackson kept three Federal armies tied up in the Valley and thereby helped to stymie Union General McClellan's Peninsular Campaign on Richmond with his new Army of the Potomac. During the Seven Days Battles that surged around Richmond during McClellan's campaign, Confederate General J E Johnston, one of the heroes of the First Manassas, was severely wounded. Johnston was replaced by General Robert E Lee; it was Lee who finished the job of driving the Army of the Potomac away from Richmond and, before long, out of Virginia entirely.

After tying up the enemy armies in the Shenandoah and keeping them from reinforcing McClellan, Stonewall Jackson hurried east to join Lee in the Seven Days Battles. As soon as Jackson's forces left the Shenandoah, new orders went out from Washington: the three Federal armies that had futilely chased Jackson were to be consolidated into one army under General John Pope, who was then to march South from

**Above:** *Stonewall Jackson directs his brigade at First Manassas, where he earned his nickname.*

**Below:** *Union marines, stationed to defend Washington, march outside their barracks.*

Washington and draw the Confederate army away from Richmond. But the plan was soon changed in light of Union failures in the Seven Days, and a new plan developed: McClellan was to move his forces around by water to unite with Pope; with the resulting army of 130,000 men, the Federals would descend into Virginia to annihilate Lee's army of 50,000. Federal intelligence estimates had more than doubled Lee's actual numbers; in contrast, Lee had a per-

**Opposite top:** *Confederate artillery repels a Union attack at First Manassas.*

**Opposite bottom:** *Rebel Black Horse Cavalry under assault by Union Zouaves.*

**Above:** *Artist Alfred R Waud sketched Union General McClellan crossing Bull Run on 29 March 1862.*

**Right:** *General George B McClellan would regain command of the Union army after Second Manassas.*

fectly clear idea of the daunting prospect he was up against. It was the first great challenge of his career.

The new commander of the Confederate Army of Northern Virginia was an unusual man for a soldier. So soft-spoken, courtly, and religious was Lee that many of his soldiers dubbed him "Granny." It was not long before they saw him more accurately: this mild-mannered Virginian aristocrat was one of the most aggressive and brilliant fighting generals who ever lived. But it is a strange position he occupies. Later called by Winston Churchill "the greatest of Americans," Lee was a primary leader of a rebellion that aimed to destroy the United States. Yet he believed neither in slavery nor in secession, and was certainly patriotic enough before the war. Like many Americans of that era, Lee placed loyalty to this home state above loyalty to the United States. In his resignation from the US Army, Lee said he could not raise his hand against Virginians; if they seceded, so must he.

It was not long before Lee was virtually deified by his Army of Northern Virginia. Moreover, the Army of Northern Virginia had an outstanding staff of subordinates. The great Stonewall Jackson was known as Lee's right arm. In addition there were the over-cautious but hard-fighting James Longstreet, impetuous A P Hill, choleric Daniel H Hill, and 25-year-old Jeb Stuart, one of the greatest cavalry-men of all time, who ful-

**Left:** *General Robert E Lee in his preferred uniform – that of a cavalry colonel. As commander of the Confederate Army of Northern Virginia, he was almost deified by his men.*

**Opposite above:** *At Cedar Mountain, in the first battle of the Second Manassas campaign, A P Hill halted a Union advance under Nathaniel Banks on 9 August.*

filled his function of being the eyes of Lee's army with extraordinary effectiveness and dash.

Such generals combined with a fighting body of the highest spirit made for one of the great armies of history, one already legendary during its own brief existence. But it is also true that there were deep and abiding weaknesses in both the command structure and army. Chief among these weaknesses was that both Lee and the Confederate government paid too little attention to logistics, especially the need to feed and clothe the army properly. For much of the war Southern soldiers marched and fought hungry, ragged, and often shoeless, even when the Confederacy had abundant supplies. The availability of arms and powder was remarkably dependable throughout the war, but soldiers need more than weapons to fight. Beyond that, Lee often gave vague orders, leaving much leeway for his generals; with a subordinate of genius like Stonewall Jackson, the results could be spectacular, but with lesser generals there were often misunderstandings. And Lee arguably gave too much of his

attention to his beloved home state of Virginia, leaving large-scale strategy to the unreliable attentions of Jefferson Davis (though this was more the fault of Davis than of Lee).

But all these things were unknown in July of 1862. By then Lee had driven McClellan from the gates of Richmond, but he faced the prospect of a grand combination of McClellan and Pope's forces that would, if successfully accomplished, spell almost certain doom for the Confederacy. On 14 July Pope began moving his forces south in Virginia, intending to take over the railroad junction at Gordonsville and then attack Lee, who for the moment was still protecting the Confederate capital from further efforts by McClellan. An observer watched Lee as he grappled with this daunting situation:

When contemplating any great undertaking or a vast strategic combination, General Lee had an abstracted manner that was altogether unlike his usual one. He would seek some level sward and pace mechanically up and down with the regularity of a sentinel on his beat; his head would

be bent as if in deep meditation, while his left hand unconsciously stroked his thick iron-grey beard.

Soon Stonewall Jackson was summoned; Lee now knew what he was going to do. Jackson and A P Hill were ordered north with 24,000 men to confront Pope and draw him away from the safety of Washington. Above all Pope had to be dealt with before McClellan could reinforce him, and time was running short it that was to be done. As always, Lee had examined his opponent carefully and knew his man. In this case, he knew he was dealing not with a worthy opponent but with a blustering fool. This may be seen in Pope's first address to his new command, in which he crowed, "Let us understand each other. I come to you from the West, where we have always seen the backs of our enemies." Lee took an uncharacteristically angry attitude towards this particular opponent; the "miscreant" Pope, Lee said, must be "suppressed."

Jackson set off with his and Hill's divisions to execute Lee's orders. He first planned to smash Pope's vanguard at Culpeper, Virginia, then to defeat the rest in detail, one corps at a time. But due to unwonted slowness, Jackson fumbled this initial strategy. On 9 August the advancing Confederates found themselves opposed by General Nathaniel Banks at Cedar Mountain. The Federals came on strongly and pushed Jackson's men back, but a crashing counterattack by A P Hill ended the enemy advance.

Pope's advance had been slowed, but no more. And now McClellan began pulling his Army of the Potomac away from Richmond by water and moving to combine with Pope. The immediate threat to the capitol over, Lee moved with Longstreet's division to join Jackson and march to the east of Pope's army, trying to maneuver to a position between him and both Washington and McClellan. This plan miscarried; because of poor staff work and a surprise attack on Jeb

**Below:** *General John Pope commanded Union forces at Second Manassas. General Lee considered him an unworthy opponent.*

**Overleaf:** *Federal troops, protected by a determined rear guard, begin their retreat at First Manassas.*

**Right:** *A column of Federal cavalry along the Rappahannock River in Virginia in August 1862.*

**Below:** *A Union brigade fails in its attempt to force strongly entrenched Confederate troops from the woods at the battle of Cedar Mountain.*

Stuart's camp (18 August) that captured Lee's plans, the Confederates were unable to march east of Pope. Finally both armies came to rest facing one another across the Rappahannock River, both making probing attacks with their cavalry. The report came to Lee that McClellan was now five days away from the juncture with Pope. In effect, the Confederates were racing with McClellan to get to Pope first. At that critical juncture in the history of the Confederacy, the combination of Lee and Jackson first revealed the genius for which history remembers them.

For the first, but not the last, time, Lee contradicted an ancient and virtually ironbound rule of military strategy: do not divide forces in the face of the enemy. In this case, it was an enemy that outnumbered Lee 75,000 to 55,000. The extraordinary bold plan was this: holding Pope in place on the Rappahannock with Longstreet's thinly spaced forces, Lee sent Jackson and Jeb Stuart on a wide envelopment, first northwest, then east, around Pope's army. Jackson's command left on 25 August; his foot soldiers duplicated the feats of marching they had demonstrated in the Valley Campaign, when they earned the title "foot cavalry." On the first day they marched 26 miles, the second day 36 miles.

At least McClellan had the sense to expect the unexpected from Stonewall Jackson. In the ensuing days that led up to the convulsion of the battle of Second Manassas, General Pope resolutely refused to believe that Jackson was behaving in anything but a timid and predictable fashion.

Pope's first surprise came on the evening of 27 August, when Jackson's men swamped the Union supply dump at Manassas. There the hungry Confederates had themselves the feast of a lifetime. After torching the remaining supplies, Jackson and Stuart pulled their forces away and, as far as Federal intelligence was concerned, vanished into thin air. General Pope, finding Jackson unexpectedly on his rear and the Federal supply line at Manassas destroyed, pulled his army away to the north on 26 August. This was what Lee had been waiting for; he took Longstreet's corps away from the Rappahannock, marching to meet Jackson. Meanwhile, Pope's blustering confusions continued; insisting that Jackson was retreating toward the Shenandoah Valley, Pope vowed to find and destroy him. Finally the Union army of 75,000 men was concentrated squarely between Jackson's force of 24,000 and Longstreet's still-distant 30,000. Here was a golden opportunity for the North: crush Jackson and then

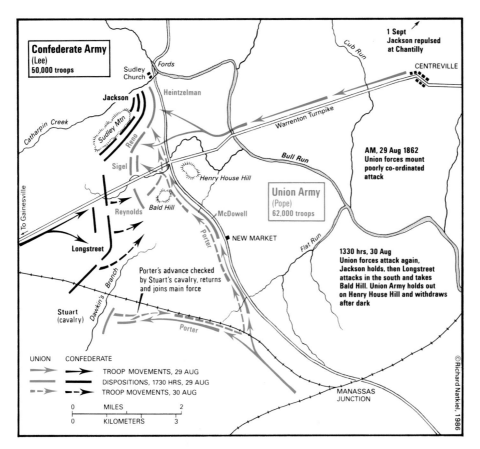

**Left:** *Map of Confederate and Union positions and movements at the Second Manassas.*

**Opposite:** *An A R Waud sketch of the defeat of the Federal Army of the Potomac under General Pope at the Second Manassas on 30 August 1862.*

turn on Longstreet. The trouble was, Pope could not find Jackson, despite frantic efforts to do so. Too, from start to very near finish, Pope ignored Longstreet entirely.

Nonetheless, with a large enemy between their divided forces the Confederates were in a desperate situation, one that might well have proven fatal if their opponent had possessed a modicum of sense. Jackson's problem was: how to hold Pope at bay until Longstreet arrived, how to attack, if possible, and still leave room to retreat. About 27 August Jackson found the place to do both those things – an unfinished railroad cut at the foot of Stony Ridge. It was an ideal defensive position, attackers having to make their way across a deep excavation. Behind the cut were mountain passes serviceable for retreat. On 27-28 August Jackson moved his forces to that position circuitously, in three detachments, and then literally hid his army in the woods behind the railroad cut.

On 28 August the Federals were in Groveton, unaware of Jackson's presence nearby. At that point Jackson made a historic gamble, a bigger one than Lee had made in dividing his army. With less than a third of the forces of the enemy, Jackson moved out and attacked the Federals, thereby revealing his position. It was a decision so bold as to seem foolhardy. The reason for it was that Jackson wanted to make sure Pope stayed away from strong defenses at nearby Centreville; if they pulled back to that position, the Federals could wait for the oncoming McClellan with impunity.

So Jackson moved out and struck the Federals near Groveton. A fierce skirmish developed as Pope turned his army to smash the supposedly retreating Jackson, meanwhile sending telegrams to Washington proclaiming victory over Jackson and saying Lee was in precipitate retreat to Richmond. Some of his officers tried to warn him of Longstreet's approach; Pope refused to listen. Now the Confederates were ready to engage the enemy before McClellan could arrive. The stage was set for the Battle of Second Manassas.

On the morning of 29 August 1862, General Pope threw 62,000 men against 20,000 Confederates, most of whom were again entrenched behind the railroad cut. All morning long the Union attacks continued; all were driven back with heavy losses. But the Confederates were increasingly desperate as the morning wore on.

As ammunition ran out, the Confederate defenders began hurling rocks at the attackers. General Maxcy Gregg walked up and down behind his troops, a sword of Revolutionary vintage in his hand, shouting "Let us die here, my men, let us die here!" Then, at about 11 in the morning, Longstreet's corp arrived on the Confederate right. In fact, Longstreet was squarely athwart a large gap in the Federal line; he could have fallen on the Union flank with devastating effect. But as was to be the case so often in the future, Longstreet was overcautious, worried about the Union corps on this right. Rather than mounting a fullscale attack, then, Longstreet moved some men over to make a demonstration on the Federal center. This sufficed to relieve the pressure on Jackson and to ensure the failure of Pope's offensive.

At the end of the day on 29 August Jackson pulled back from some of his advanced positions. Obtuse as ever, Pope declared that Jackson was retreating (the Federal commander was still oblivious to the presence of Longstreet). Pope ordered his men to pursue the enemy the next day. Lee encouraged Pope's illusions by letting some carefully-misinformed Federal prisoners escape back to their own lines; these returned prisoners assured Pope that the enemy was indeed retreating.

Next day, 30 August, the Federals, renewed their assault on the Southern lines, which now contained the entire Army of Northern Virginia. Lee let Pope hit Jackson's left, then sent Longstreet against the opposite Union flank. Longstreet remembered that morning:

A heavy fire of shot and shell was being poured into the thick column of the enemy, and in ten minutes their stubborn masses began to waver and give back. For a moment there was chaos; then order returned and they re-formed, apparently to renew the attack. Meanwhile my other eight pieces reported to me, and from the crest of the little hill the fire of twelve guns cut them down. As the cannon thundered the ranks broke, only to be formed again with dogged determination. A third time the batteries tore the Federals to pieces, and as they fell back under this terrible fire, I sprung everything to the charge. My troops leaped forward with exultant yells, and all along the line we pushed forward.

Now the Federal army was pincered between Longstreet and Jackson. Lee proceeded to swing his forces shut around the enemy like a gate.

Pope and his army were routed, but a stout Federal defense at Henry House Hill saved the army and made an orderly retreat possible. Lee and Jackson had created the first great victory of their immortal partnership.

There was much more to their success than a battle won, however. The Seven Days Battles, Jackson's Shenandoah Valley Campaign and the Second Manassas had really been one gigantic and ultimately victorious campaign of three months' duration. In that time Lee had sent two enormous Federal armies running back to Washington and virtually cleared Virginia of enemy forces. When Lee took command the North had been at the gates of Richmond. Now Lee was only 25 miles from Washington.

Yet in the end, the Second Manassas proved to be an incomplete victory. After driving the North from the field Lee tried to maintain the offensive, sending the corps of Jackson and Longstreet around the Federal west flank at Centreville. In this effort the exhausted Rebels discovered their enemy was still ready to fight. Jackson struck the Federals, but they resisted strongly even after two corps commanders were killed. In the end the Federals got away to Washington. On the next day Pope's forces were merged into McClellan's command, and that general once again took over operations in the East. Pope was never to command in the field again.

The Second Manassas was the first really devastating engagement of the Civil War. Now the soldiers and civilians of the contending nations were to learn the real costs of war. Confederate casualties were 1481 killed, 7627 wounded, 89 missing, a total of 9197 out of 48,527 engaged – 19 percent casualties. Federal losses were 1724 killed, 8372 wounded, 5958 missing, a total of 16,054 of the 75,696 engaged – 21 percent casualties.

Now Lee had to do something. He could not stay put; his army was in an exposed position near the enemy capital, where there were enormous masses of soldiers who would sooner or later be coming at him again. Lee knew he did not have sufficient strength to mount a siege of Washington. But it was not in his nature to pull back to safety near Richmond. Lee was above all an aggressive general; thus he decided to keep going, to invade Maryland. In this decision he underestimated his enemy and overestimated his own men. It was Pope, not the Federal soldiers, who had lost the Second Manassas; in battle the Northern men had fought with the same valor as their enemy.

# JACKSON'S VALLEY CAMPAIGN

**S**tonewall Jackson showed his mettle in the Battle of Second Manassas. It was one of his greatest moments, but it was an earlier campaign in the Shenandoah Valley of Virginia that has forever stamped Jackson's genius in the annals of military history.

Thomas Jonathan Jackson had not seemed so promising at the outset of his military career. He arrived at West Point an awkward, taciturn mountain boy clad in rough homespun. With great effort he managed to rise from the bottom to nearly the top of his class during his four years. When the

**Right:** *Union General John Charles Frémont, commander of the Frederal Mountain Division in western Virginia, was defeated by Jackson in the Shenandoah Valley Campaign.*

**Opposite:** *General Thomas Jonathan ("Stonewall") Jackson, one of the greatest generals of the Civil War. His death on 10 May 1863 was a devastating blow to the Confederate cause.*

Civil War began he was a professor of mathematics and natural philosophy at the Virginia Military Institute and was already viewed as a strange character. He was a fanatical, brooding, and humorless Presbyterian, who never smoked or drank or played cards. He was obsessed with his health and with eccentric remedies: during the war he sucked lemons constantly, shunned pepper, claiming it made his left leg weak, and kept his right arm raised a good deal of the time, saying it improved the circulation.

So peculiar was Jackson that some of his own subordinates questioned his sanity. His obsessive secrecy drove his men close to madness themselves; not only did the enemy never know where Jackson was going, neither did any of his command, much of the time. But it was not long before everyone on both sides understood the military genius of Stonewall Jackson, and thereafter his men were happy to accept any

odd notion he devised. He was to become the indispensible right arm of Robert E. Lee, who described Jackson thus:

> A man he is of contrasts so complete that he appears one day a Presbyterian deacon who delights in theological discussion and, the next, a reincarnated Joshua. He lives by the New Testament and fights by the Old.

The Shenandoah Valley of Virginia was one of the vitally important stretches of land in the Confederacy. It is the most fertile farmland imaginable, and was thus the breadbasket of the South. Beyond that, it was the ideal route for Confederate armies marching North for Maryland or Pennsylvania. To the Union, the Shenandoah was strategically useless; marching south in it took them nowhwere in particular. The Valley was important to the north only because it was so important to

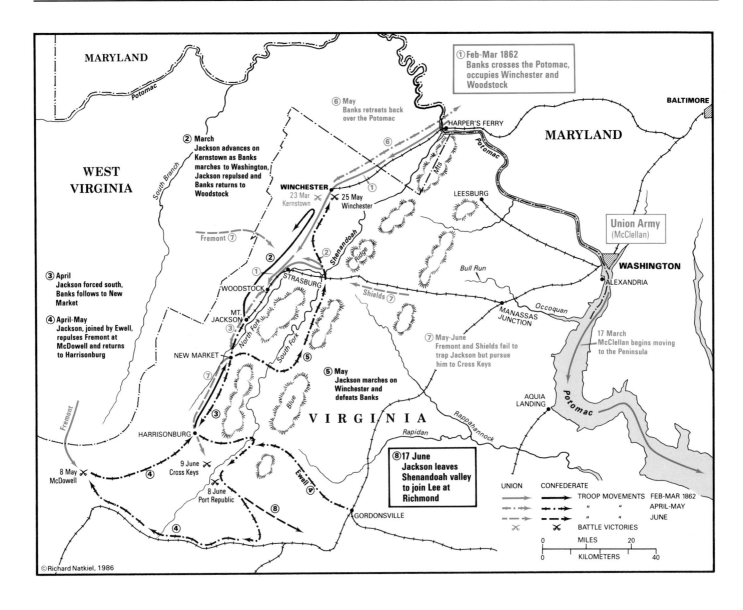

MARYLAND

WEST VIRGINIA

① Feb-Mar 1862
Banks crosses the Potomac,
occupies Winchester and
Woodstock

⑥ May
Banks retreats back
over the Potomac

BALTIMORE

HARPER'S FERRY

MARYLAND

② March
Jackson advances on
Kernstown as Banks
marches to Washington,
Jackson repulsed and
Banks returns to
Woodstock

LEESBURG

WINCHESTER
23 Mar Kernstown    × 25 May Winchester

Fremont ⑦

③ April
Jackson forced south,
Banks follows to New
Market

STRASBURG

WOODSTOCK

④ April-May
Jackson, joined by Ewell,
repulses Fremont at
McDowell and returns
to Harrisonburg

MT. JACKSON

NEW MARKET

Bull Run

Union Army
(McClellan)

WASHINGTON

ALEXANDRIA

Shields ⑦

MANASSAS JUNCTION

Occoquan

17 March
McClellan begins moving
to the Peninsula

⑤ May
Jackson marches on
Winchester and
defeats Banks

⑦ May-June
Fremont and Shields fail to
trap Jackson but pursue
him to Cross Keys

AQUIA LANDING

Fremont

HARRISONBURG

V I R G I N I A

Rappahannock

Rapidan

⑧ 17 June
Jackson leaves
Shenandoah valley
to join Lee at
Richmond

8 May McDowell

9 June Cross Keys

8 June Port Republic

Ewell ④

GORDONSVILLE

UNION    CONFEDERATE

TROOP MOVEMENTS FEB-MAR 1862
"           "    APRIL-MAY
"           "    JUNE

BATTLE VICTORIES

0        MILES        20
0     KILOMETERS      40

© Richard Natkiel, 1986

the Confederacy. Thus in October 1861 a Federal army occupied Romney, in the northern part of the Valley, and threatened Winchester; the Union was preparing to clear the Shenandoah of Confederates. In response, Stonewall Jackson and his brigade were sent to take charge of operations in the Shenandoah. With his Stonewall Brigade, some militia, and other troops, Jackson (now a major-general) commanded around 10,000 men. The main Union forces in the area were some 10,000 men under General Nathaniel P Banks.

After a winter of mostly fruitless maneuvering by both sides, Bank occupied Winchester in March of 1862, chasing Jackson's forces away and sending a Federal division south to occupy Strasburg. From that position Banks prepared to leave the Valley and join General McClellan's Federal Army of the Potomac, which was marching towards Richmond.

On 21 March Jackson learned of the planned Federal move from his cavalry commander, Turner Ashby. It was clear to Jackson as it was to his superiors that this must not happen: if Banks or any other major Union forces joined McClellan (a Federal army under McDowell was just east of the Valley and also slated to reinforce McClellan) they would gain overwhelming strength, and the Confederacy would be doomed. Lee, who at that time was overseeing operations in Virginia rather than commanding in the field, ordered Jackson to make a strategic diversion to keep Union forces, especially Banks's and McDowell's, in the Shenandoah and away from McClellan. In the process, he was to try to lead the Union high command into scattering their armies and also defend Rich-

mond from the west. In all those requirements Jackson was to prove successful beyond anyone's expectations.

Hurrying to keep the Federals in place, Jackson ordered Ashby's cavalry to attack Shields's division of Banks's army at Kernstown on 22 March 1862.

Next day Jackson arrived and followed up with his infantry (after searching his soul about fighting on Sunday). The Confederate attack went well for a while, until Shields moved some concealed forces into line. Then, outnumbered and low on ammunition, Jackson's men retreated, with Ashby covering the rear. Casualties in the fighting were disproportionate: the South had lost 700 of 4200 engaged; the Union 590 of 9000 engaged. It seemed a most unpromising beginning for Jackson's campaign.

In fact, Kernstown proved to be as good as a major victory for the South. Federal authorities assumed that Jackson's command was far larger than it actually was, and simply threw over the entire plan to reinforce McClellan, to that general's great disgust (for all his mistakes, McClellan understood better than his superiors in Washington that Jackson's campaign was a diversion). Orders went out from Washington: Banks and McDowell were to stay in the Shenandoah to deal with Jackson; indeed, some additional troops were stripped from McClellan for the purpose. At length there were three uncoordinated Federal commands trying to clear the Shenandoah Valley – Banks, McDowell, and, to the west, the army of John C Frémont.

As the Federal armies prepared to pursue him, Jackson

**Opposite:** *Troop movements in the Valley Campaign, February–June 1862.*

**Right:** *General Richard S Ewell led a division of Confederates in Jackson's Valley Campaign.*

**Below:** *Union General Frémont taking command of the Department of the West. He was removed for political and military errors but, owing to his popularity, was reassigned to western Virginia.*

withdrew gradually up the Valley (that is, to the south) with his 6000 men; Banks cautiously followed with 15,000. Then Jackson suddenly made a forced march to Swift Run Gap, in the eastern mountains. There his command was on the flank of Banks's army at Harrisonburg. Banks thus could not continue on up the Valley, for Jackson would be behind him, on the Union supply line. At Swift Run Gap in late April, Jackson was reinforced by 8000 men including the command of General Richard S Ewell; added to earlier reinforcements, this brought Rebel strength to 17,000 (which was as high as it would be in the campaign).

Of course the Federals were not standing still; Frémont began moving his forces east to join Banks in operating against Jackson. Learning of this Jackson made plans to stop that conjunction, which would likely to be fatal to his efforts. As he would so often in the future, Lee wisely gave Jackson fre rein. With a series of brilliant and lightning-quick maneuvers Jackson began his momentous campaign.

Leaving Ewell at Swift Run Gap to keep Banks in place, and sending Ashby's cavalry to make some feinting attacks, Jackson moved to strike Frémont's advance. In the most rigorous secrecy the Confederates began their march. Only Jackson knew that his destination was the town of McDowell, where R H Milroy's division was just pulling in. Driving his troops in continuous forced marches, Jackson moved to the attack. So fast did his men march that they began to be called "foot

cavalry"; they made 92 miles in four days of wet and muddy weather. On 7 May they drove Federal outposts back into McDowell. There the Federal command numbered some 6000, under Milroy and Schenck, to Jackson's 10,000. With classic skill, Jackson had maneuvered his small army to gain local superiority over his enemy.

On 8 May 1962, the Federals took the initiative at McDowell, attacking in the afternoon. Despite heavy losses, the Confederates repulsed the attack and sent the Yankees running west. Though the wet weather and enemy resistance made pursuit most difficult, the Rebels managed to chase their enemy to Franklin, West Virginia. Then Jackson withdrew, using Ashby's cavalry as a screen. The South had lost 498 men to the Union's 256, but they had won the day. Jackson, however, was by no means ready to rest. On 14 May he marched his command for Harrisonburg.

As the Confederates marched, Banks dug his army in at Strasburg and sent troops to reinforce General McDowell to the east. Thus Banks left himself with only 8000 men, a most dangerous position to be in with Stonewall Jackson around. At that point Jackson seemed, as far as the Federals were concerned, to disappear from the face of the earth. Feinting at Banks with cavalry, Jackson took the bulk of his forces east, crossed the Massanutten Mountains in the middle of the Valley, joined Ewell (making a total then of 16,000 men) and, after marching up to 30 miles a day with his "foot cavalry,"

pounced on a Federal garrison of 1000 at Front Royal on 23 May.

Confederate General Richard Taylor remembered the approach to Front Royal:

> Past midday . . . there rushed out of the wood to meet us a young, rather well-looking woman, afterward widely known as [Southern spy] Belle Boyd. Breathless with speed and agitation, some time elapsed before she found her voice. Then, with much volubility, she said we were near Front Royal, beyond the wood; that the town was filled with Federals, whose camp was on the west side of the river, where they had guns in position . . . that they believed Jackson to be west of Massanutten . . . that General Banks, the Federal commander, was at Winchester . . . where he was slowly concentrating his widely scattered forces to meet Jackson's advance, which was expected some days later.

Shocked by Jackson's surprise attack, the Federals at Front Royal withdrew toward Strasburg; but it was hopeless – by the end of the day the Union had lost 904 of 1063 men in the garrison, most of them captured. The Confederates had fewer than 50 casualties. Jackson had again concentrated to outnumber an outlying enemy detachment and won the day. Now he had to figure out what Banks was going to do next – stay put in Strasburg, go west to join Frémont, go north to strong positions at Winchester, or retreat east to safety near Washington. Deciding finally that Banks would probably stay put or go east, Jackson began marching to Middletown, near Strasburg.

Banks for once, did not move as expected by his enemy. After learning of the disaster at Front Royal, Banks pulled his army back to Winchester, arriving on 24 May. Hearing word of the Federal move, Jackson saw its potential for trouble – knowing the area as he did, Jackson knew the town had high ground and would be impossible to assault if the Yankees settled in. So once again, he drove his "foot cavalry" hard. At first, the exhausted Confederates dallied, wasting time looting a captured supply train, but then they marched all night and reached Winchester just after midnight.

At dawn on 25 May 1862 the Confederates drove in the Fed-

**Above:** *A "trooper" in Jackson's famous "foot cavalry," noted for their marching ability.*

**Right:** *A corps of Confederates fends off an attack from advancing Pennsylvania Bucktails in woods near Harrisonburg on 7 June 1862.*

eral pickets, and the battle of Winchester was on. For a time the Union cavalry and artillery kept the Rebels at bay; then Jackson put men on the Federal right flank, and Ewell worked his division around to the left flank. Jackson thereupon advanced his center and right together, and the Federals broke and ran. Banks withdrew under pursuit across the Potomac and out of the campaign for good. Between the defeats at Front Royal and Winchester, Banks lost some 3000 men of the 8500 in his command; Jackson's losses in the same period were about 400 of 16,000.

With these extraordinary achievements under their belts, the Confederates rested a couple of days before taking the road again. They then marched north to concentrate near Harpers Ferry. One of Jackson's opponents admiringly summarized Jackson's achievements so far:

As the result of these operations, Milroy and Schenck were now beaten, Banks's army was routed, the fertile Valley of Virginia cleared of Union troops, Harpers Ferry in danger and Maryland . . . threatened. In addition Washington was thrown into alarm and trepidation; McDowell's movement to connect with McClellan was suspended; he was ordered to move 20,000 men into the Valley to cut off Jackson, while Frémont with his whole force was ordered into the Valley at Harrisonburg for the same purpose. The whole plan of Union operations had been completely upset, and confusion reigned from

one end of the line to the other. At no time during the war was there such dismay in the North. . . . General Jackson himself seems to have been the only one who had not lost his head. He kept his army from May 26 to May 30 threatening Harpers Ferry and an invasion of Maryland.

In deciding to devote the efforts of these commands to chasing Jackson instead of reinforcing McClellan near Richmond, the Washington authorities made one of the great blunders of the conflict, quite possibly prolonging the war for three years. All this because of the brooding, brilliant Jackson and his small band of rugged soldiers.

Of course Jackson had planned everything to achieve just

that end. But his problems were by no means over. Now he had simultaneously to keep the Federals in the Valley busy, ship east the enormous quantities of supplies he had captured, and pull back from the Harpers Ferry area to avoid being trapped by the converging advances of Frémont and McDowell. Leaving the Stonewall Brigade to keep Banks in check, Jackson began pulling the rest of his forces south on 30 May. Things quickly came to a head. Jackson was riding on a railway train in front of his troops when a courier stopped the engine to tell Jackson that McDowell had recaptured Front Royal. The two Federal armies were moving in faster than expected, and Confederate forces were spread out around the Valley. Calmly Jackson issued his orders.

**Left:** *Colonel Turner Ashby, Jackson's cavalry commander, was killed in an engagement near Harrisonburg on 6 June.*

**Below:** *Virginia infantry encamped in the woods near Leesburg.*

The cavalry under Turner Ashby were sent to stop Federal's advance; an infantry detachment did likewise with McDowell's men at Front Royal. By 1 June, Jackson had pulled 15,000 men, 200 prisoners, and a double wagon-train seven miles long safely out of Strasburg; 50,000 Federals had not been able to corral them. Jackson then moved south up the Shenandoah Valley, burning bridges as he went. On 2 June Federal cavalry hit Jackson's rear guard, but Ashby delayed the Yankees long enough to give the Rebel infantry a day's lead. On 6 June came another Federal strike; this time the gallant Ashby was killed, but the Federal advance came to little – Union reinforcements could not move up because the Confederates had destroyed the bridges.

But by next day Jackson was in the worst spot of the entire campaign, squarely between two converging enemy columns. With customary boldness, he moved out to take the offensive from his position at Port Republic. On 7 June the Confederates tried without luck to draw Frémont out before McDowell arrived. Next morning a Federal detachment got into Port Republic and nearly captured Jackson – this was Shields's advance, part of McDowell's command moving up from the east. Meanwhile, Frémont moved to attack from the west. It appeared to be the end for Jackson.

Yet the Federal push became muddled, mostly due, once again, to the bridges Jackson had so carefully burned. On 8 June the Federals moved forward at Cross Keys, but were driven back and pursued; in that action Ewell's division of 6500 bested Frémont's 10,500. On the next day Jackson held Frémont at bay with Ewell and moved to attack Shields's 3000 men at Port Republic.

On the morning of 9 June the Stonewall Brigade hit the Federal right, while others attacked the enemy left. But the Confederate attacks were beaten back, and Ewell was slow to move over in support. Ewell's advance forces were then sent on an envelopment of the Federal left; this failed too, but at last the rest of Ewell's men came up. CSA General Richard Taylor remembered what happened next:

> Wheeling to the right, with colors advanced, like a solid wall [the enemy] marched straight upon us. There seemed nothing left but to set our backs to the mountain and die hard. At the instant, crashing through the underwood, came Ewell, outriding staff and escort. He produced the effect of a reinforcement, and was welcomed with cheers. The line before us halted and threw forward skirmishers. A

moment later, a shell came shrieking along it, loud Confederate cheers reached our delighted ears, and Jackson, freed from his toils, rushed up like a whirlwind, the enemy in rapid retreat.

Shields and his outnumbered Federal forces retreated in good order, fighting as they went. Frémont had been unable to help due to yet another burned bridge. In two days of battle Frémont had suffered 684 casualties of 17,000 engaged; at Port Republic the Federals lost 1018. The total Southern casualties were about 1100 of 16,000 engaged. Jackson had once again defeated his enemy in detail, one division at a time. In fact, in a month of campaigning against vastly superior total Federal forces he had outnumbered his enemy in nearly every individual engagement.

With his extraordinary campaign in the Shenandoah Valley completed and the entire Federal war effort in turmoil and confusion, Jackson now marched east to join Lee in the Seven Days Battles and the Second Manassas. In one month Jackson's army had marched more than 250 miles, fought four pitched battles and endless skirmishes and had captured more than 400 prisoners and enormous quantities of arms and supplies. Jackson had brilliantly followed his own maxims of war:

> Always mystify, mislead, and surprise the enemy, if possible; and when you strike and overcome him, never let up in the pursuit so long as your men have strength to follow; for an army routed, if hotly pursued, becomes panic-stricken, and can then be destroyed by half their number. The other rule is, never fight against heavy odds, if by any possible maneuvering you can hurl your own force on only a part, and that the weakest part, of your enemy and crush it. Such tactics will win every time, and a small army may thus destroy a large one in detail, and repeated victory will make it invincible.

Stonewall Jackson's tactics of speed and secrecy have been studied by military men ever since (for example, these lessons were not lost on the Nazis in preparing their *Blitzkreig* of World War II). But the immediate effect on Southern fortunes in the Civil War was direct and profound. Jackson had played a remarkable chess game and had checkmated his enemy. Now the impetus of the war in the Eastern Theater was firmly on the Confederate side.

**Right:** *A Confederate camp in the Shenandoah Valley.*

# FREDERICKSBURG

On 3 September 1862 Lee proposed to Jefferson Davis that the Confederacy capitalize on its great victory at Second Manassas by mounting an immediate invasion of Maryland. In theory, there was much to recommend this bold stroke. The Union Army of the Potomac was injured and off balance, and, because a Confederate thrust into Maryland would indirectly threaten Washington, McClellan would be kept fully on the defensive and would be incapable of any meaningful counter-strokes into Virginia. Also, Lee and the South in general had high hopes that a Confederate military presence in Maryland would cause many citizens of that crucial border state to rally to the Confederate cause and perhaps even

prompt the whole state to secede. Finally, and perhaps most important, a successful offensive into the North might well clinch the Confederacy's continuing efforts to gain diplomatic recognition from Great Britain and France, thus assuring the South of a badly needed infusion of foreign capital, weapons and supplies.

Attractive as all these strategic objectives were, they were predicated on some large assumptions, and indications that the assumptions may have been too large began appearing almost as soon as the Army of Northern Virginia crossed over into Maryland early in September. Marylanders did *not* hasten to throw in their lot with the CSA; indeed, they gave Lee's

army a generally chilly reception. Worse, McClellan seemed to be pulling his Union forces together remarkably efficiently and to be moving with unaccustomed dispatch toward another major confrontation.

That confrontation took place at Sharpsburg, near Antietam Creek, less than two weeks after the Maryland invasion had begun, so soon, indeed, that Lee barely had time to assemble his scattered forces to receive the shock. (But for McClellan's last-minute dawdling, Lee probably would not have had time; but then, Lee knew his dilatory opponent well.) Hostilities began early in the morning of 17 September and raged confusedly and indecisively throughout a day that would prove to be the single bloodiest in the entire Civil War. When it was over, Lee for the first time had not won a decisive victory in a major encounter. True, his army was still very much intact, but there was no denying that it had been much harmed. The number of dead, wounded and missing on each side was about the same – something over 12,000 apiece – but as a percentage of those engaged, the South's losses were much higher – on the order of 26 percent, as opposed to the Union's 16 percent.

Although the South had consistently displayed superior generalship in the battle, Antietam ended as a tactical stalemate and a strategic reversal for the Confederacy. None of the objectives of the now-stymied invasion had been achieved, and when, in the aftermath of the battle, Lincoln issued his Emancipation Proclamation, thus formally making slavery a war issue, the Confederacy's hopes of receiving foreign diplomatic recognition became even more remote, for now not even the South's best European friends wanted to appear to be on the side of slavery.

After the convulsion of Antietam the two great armies of the East rested, licking their wounds. Nonetheless, the processes of planning, raiding, and reconnaissance continued: in early October, Jeb Stuart and his Southern cavalrymen raided completely around the Army of the Potomac, as they had done before, during the Peninsular Campaign. President Lincoln goaded McClellan to action, and the general reluct-

**Left:** *The Battle of Antietam, 17 September 1862. Union troops crossing Burnside Bridge are met by withering Rebel fire.*

**Above:** *A soldier in the uniform of the Maryland Guard.*

**Overleaf:** *Soldiers and wagons on the bridge at Antietam Creek.*

antly put his army in motion to the south – as always, with maddening caution. Lincoln had seen it before; McClellan, Lincoln had cracked, was chronically infected with "the slows." This time, however, the president had had enough. Lincoln was not fooled into thinking Antietam a victory, as most of the North thought it. Now his general had returned to his inchworm mode of campaigning. On 7 November 1862, Lincoln removed McClellan from command. It was undoubtedly a long overdue change. But as McClellan's replacement Lincoln made a most unfortunate choice – General Ambrose E Burnside, who happened to be one of the most inept generals of all time.

A genial handsome man, Burnside sported an extravagant set of muttonchop whiskers which were perhaps his most enduring legacy – they gave the word "sideburns" to the language. Perhaps the secret of his success was that "Burn," as he was affectionately known, *looked* the way most folks thought a general should look. Favoring the appointment as well, from the president's point of view, was the fact that Burnside had no political ambitions, as McClellan certainly did (McClellan was to challenge Lincoln for the presidency in the next election). As to Burnside's generalship – Grant later wrote that he was "an officer who was generally liked and respected. He was not, however, fitted to command an army. No one knew better than himself."

When Burnside assumed command, his Army of the Potomac was near Warrenton, Virginia, nearly between Jackson's and Longstreet's divisions, Jackson then being in the Shenandoah Valley and Longstreet at Culpeper. Instead of striking

**Left:** *The Emancipation Proclamation, proposed five days after Antietam.*

**Below:** *Jeb Stuart crosses the Potomac, October 1862.*

**Opposite:** *The Battle of Fredericksburg, 13 December 1862. General Burnside wasted his Federal forces in frontal assaults on the entrenched enemy.*

# PLAN of the BATTLE of FREDERICKSBURG

## DECEMBER 13TH 1862

MILES

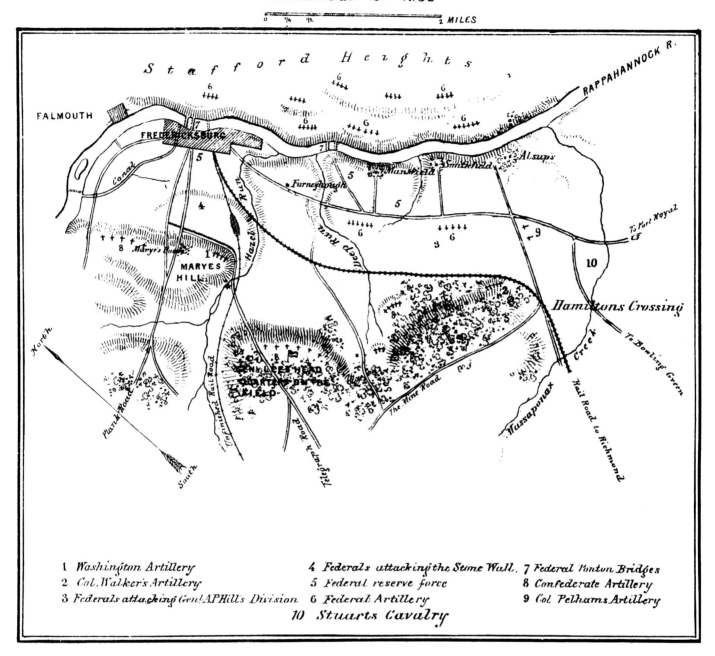

1 Washington Artillery    4 Federals attacking the Stone Wall.    7 Federal Ponton Bridges
2 Col. Walker's Artillery    5 Federal reserve force    8 Confederate Artillery
3 Federals attacking Genl. APHill's Division    6 Federal Artillery    9 Col. Pelhams Artillery
10 Stuarts Cavalry.

the two enemy wings in succession, with a fair chance of defeating them in detail, Burnside simply decided to try and make a beeline for Richmond, occupying Fredericksburg on the way. This was his first blunder: his real goal should have been to conquer Lee's army, not the Rebel capital.

On 17 November, Sumner's Federal division arrived across the river from Fredericksburg, which lay on the banks of the Rappahannock. At that point Sumner could have taken the town without resistance; Longstreet's division was alerted and on the way but had not yet arrived. Making his second big mistake, Burnside did not allow Sumner to cross the river but told him to wait for the arrival of a pontoon train with which to build bridges.

Longstreet arrived on 18 November; Jackson's corps did not pull in until the 30th. During this time, when the enemy was quite vulnerable, Burnside sat on the east bank waiting for his pontoons. Arriving on the 20th, Lee sized up his opponent with his usual acumen and decided to dig his army into the heights behind Fredericksburg, and from there to await

the attack. Burnside's pontoons arrived on the 25 of November; nonetheless, he delayed his offensive until 11 December, giving the Confederates time to construct virtually invulnerable positions on high ground.

Lee had wisely picked the heights behind Fredericksburg to defend rather than the town itself. Knowing he could not prevent the Federals from crossing the Rappahannock, he positioned sharpshooters in town to slow the crossing. The Confederates had 78,500 men to Burnside's 122,000 – as always, Lee was vastly outnumbered. For the Southerners, it was a matter of nearly three weeks of waiting.

On 10 December, General Burnside issued some confusing orders, the gist of which was that five pontoon bridges were to be pushed across the river for the crossing of infantry. Longstreet remembered the effectiveness of the sharpshooters Lee had placed in the town:

On the morning of the 11th . . . the Federals came down to the river's edge and began the construction of their

**Opposite top:** *Union engineers placed these pontoon bridges across the Rappahannock River at Fredericksburg.*

**Opposite bottom:** *While some Federal troops row across the river, engineers hurry to complete a pontoon bridge.*

**Right:** *Union soldiers rest briefly in the center of Fredericksburg before attempting to assault the heights above the town.*

bridges, when Barksdale opened fire with such effect that they were forced to retire. Again and again they made an effort to cross, but each time they were met and repulsed by the well-directed bullets of the Mississippians. This contest lasted until 1 o'clock, when the Federals, with angry desperation, turned their whole available force of artillery on the little city, and sent down from the heights of a perfect storm of shot and shell, crushing the houses with a cyclone of fiery metal. . . . But, in the midst of all this fury, the little brigade of Mississippians clung to their work. At last, when I had everything in readiness, I sent a peremptory order to Barksdale to withdraw . . . before the Federals, who had by that time succeeded in landing a number of their troops. The Federals then constructed their pontoons without molestation, and during the night and the following day the grand division of Sumner passed over into Fredericksburg.

About a mile and a half below the town, where the Deep Run empties into the Rappahannock, General Franklin had been allowed without serious opposition to throw two pontoon-bridges on the 11th, and his grand division passed over . . . in front of Stonewall Jackson's corps. The 11th and 12th were thus spent by the Federals in crossing the river and preparing for battle.

During the night of the 12th, 50,000 Federals spent an uneasy bivouac around Fredericksburg, the time enlivened by a considerable amount of looting (though the valuables of the citizens had already been well picked over by the Confederates after the civilians evacuated to the hills and woods). Everyone knew that the next day would see a bloody contest indeed; and many Federals were already in despair at the prospect of assaulting the heights.

Longstreet wrote of the dawn of the 13th, which he observed from his position of command on the left wing of Lee's army:

As the mist rose, the Confederates saw the movement against their right near Hamilton's Crossing. [Artillery]

Major Pelham opened fire upon Franklin's command and gave him lively work, which was kept up until Jackson ordered Pelham to retire. Franklin then advanced rapidly to the hill where Jackson's troops had been stationed, filling the woods with shot as he progressed. Silently Jackson awaited the approach of the Federals until they were within good range, and then he opened a terrific fire which threw the Federals into some confusion. The enemy again massed and advanced, pressing through a gap between Archer and Lane. This broke Jackson's line and threatened very serious trouble. The Federals who had wedged themselves in through that gap came upon Gregg's brigade, and then the severe encounter ensued in which the latter general was mortally wounded. Archer and Lane very soon received reinforcements and, rallying, joined in the counter-attack and recovered their lost ground . . . the counter-attack drove the Federals back to the railroad and beyond the reach of our guns on the left. Some of our troops following up this repulse got too far out, and were in turn much discomfited when left to the enemy's superior numbers, and were obliged to retire in poor condition. A Federal brigade advancing under cover of Deep Run was discovered at this time and attacked by regiments of Pender's and Law's brigades. Jackson's second line advancing, the Federals were forced to retire. This series of demonstrations and attacks, the partial success and final discomfiture of the Federals, constitute the hostile movements between the Confederate right and the Federal left.

This fighting on the right had gone on for some three hours. Having been repulsed, Franklin's division sank into exhaustion. But while the Union assaults of the 13th were breaking on Lee's right, the other half of the Army of the Potomac had been crossing the river and gathering around Fredericksburg for an all-out offensive on Longstreet's position at and below Marye's Height. The first of six major Federal assaults set out about noon, heading straight for the strongest part of the Confederate line. Advancing across open ground, the Federal lines were torn by artillery fire, then came in rifle range of a line of Rebels, the brigade of General Thomas Cobb, posted in a sunken road behind a stone wall at the foot of Marye's Heights.

From Lee's Hill, above the battlefield, Longstreet watched wave after wave of Federal advance as if on parade to be torn to pieces at the foot of Marye's Heights:

> The field in front of Cobb was thickly strewn with the dead and dying Federals, but again they formed with desperate courage and renewed the attack and again were driven off. At each attack the slaughter was so great that by the time the third attack was repulsed, the ground was so thickly strewn with dead that the bodies seriously impeded the approach of the Federals.

And so it went as the long afternoon wore on, assault after hopeless and tragic assault, the Union dead and wounded pil-

ing higher before the stone wall. Late in the day, as the Federal efforts were tailing off on the left, Jackson ordered an advance on the right, but he was dissuaded due to extensive Federal artillery covering the open ground in his front. Lee had shifted a number of troops from his right to the center to meet the Union offensive, but they were scarcely necessary. As a Union soldier bitterly commented, "No troops in the world would have won a victory if placed in the position ours were. Few armies . . . would have stood as well as ours did. It can hardly be in human nature for men to show more valor, or generals to manifest less judgment, than were perceptible on our side that day." Another Yankee soldier put it more succinctly: "They may as well have tried to take Hell."

Night fell at last on the scene of carnage, and it was over for those Federals who had made their escape from Marye's Heights. But many were too wounded to move, or were trapped in front of enemy guns and hugging the ground all

**Left:** *General Humphrey's division charges into heavy fire from the Confederate defenders entrenched at the foot of Marye's Heights.*

**Left:** *General Edwin Sumner's men launch a fruitless assault on Marye's Heights, 13 December.*

night. Union officer Joshua Chamberlain wrote an unforgettable account of that night of horror:

Out of that silence [following] the battle's crash and roar rose new sounds more appalling still . . . a strange ventriloquism, of which you could not locate the source . . . a wail so far and deep and wide, as if a thousand discords were flowing together into a key-note weird, unearthly, terrible to hear and bear . . . the writhing concord broken by cries for help pierced by shrieks of paroxysm; some begging for a drop of water; some calling on God for pity; and some on friendly hands to finish what the enemy had so horribly begun; some with delirious, dreamy voices murmuring loved names, as if the dearest were bending over them. . . .

In Burnside's tragic and stupid assaults of 13 December at Fredericksburg the North had lost 12,700 killed and wounded of 106,000 committed. The South's casualties were less than half those – 5300 casualties of 72,500 engaged. During the night a Federal prisoner caught in Confederate lines produced a memorandum from Burnside ordering renewed attacks next day. Lee and Longstreet made ready to meet it. The attack never came; Burnside's staff had dissuaded him. Surveying the field that showed only dead and dying Federals and no attack, Lee joked to Longstreet. "General, I am losing confidence in your friend General Burnside." Perhaps Lee should have ordered a counterattack; but he did not know

*Above: Rebel troops view ruined Fredericksburg Bridge after the battle. The defeated Union troops withdrew across the river unopposed.*

*Overleaf: Union soldiers cross the Rappahannock as engineers rush to complete a span of a pontoon bridge before Fredericksburg.*

how stricken the Federals were, and certainly he had on his mind his army's narrow escape in the Antietam campaign.

But Burnside was not quite done yet. He made one more effort to do his job, this time by marching the Army of the Potomac upstream to cross the Rappahannock in hopes of striking Lee's flank. But this operation began squarely in the middle of the usual January thaw, with its accompanying torrents of rain. During it the entire army nearly disappeared into an apparently bottomless sea of mud. This Mud March as history dubbed it, was soon aborted, and the bedraggled and demoralized Army of the Potomac slogged back to their camps across the river from Lee at Fredericksburg. A compassionate Longstreet wrote perhaps the best epitaph for the Union dead.

The spectacle that we saw upon the battle-field was one of the most distressing I ever witnessed. The charges had been desperate and bloody, but utterly hopeless. I thought, as I saw the Federals come again and again to their death, that they deserved success if courage and daring could entitle soldiers to victory.

Intelligence concerning enemies' doings traveled slowly and tenuously in the Civil War compared with later conflicts. But news always seemed to travel faster in the direction of Robert E Lee. The Confederate commander got his information from a variety of sources – above all from Jeb Stuart's cavalry, which were the eyes of the Army of Northern Virginia; from spies in Washington and in Southern towns occupied by the Union; from Northern prisoners and deserters; and, not infrequently, from reading Northern newspapers (there was little organized censorship in Washington, and often the South could find out about enemy operations simply by perusing the daily papers).

At the end of January, 1863, Lee learned that he had a new opponent, that the Union Army of the Potomac had seen the fourth change of command in a year. Following Burnside's debacle at Fredericksburg and his being relieved at his own request, Washington gave the army to General Joseph Hooker, called "Fighting Joe" by the press. Hooker's friends in Washington had overcome political opposition to the appointment, and Hooker was one of the few generals who genuinely wanted the job – indeed, he had schemed to get it. Lee's response to this Federal change of command is not recorded. It is likely he knew his opponent's strengths and weaknesses as well as usual. If so, Lee knew that there were two Joe Hookers: one of them an experienced, dashing and hard-fighting general; the other was a man fond of criticizing his superiors and scheming for his own benefit, and equally fond of the bottle and the ladies.

But in taking command in the winter of 1863 Hooker suddenly revealed unexpected qualities as an organizer. He repaired the Army of the Potomac from the ground up, improving the food supply, hospital care, and sanitation of his

**Opposite:** *General "Fighting Joe" Hooker, depicted leading his corps at Antietam, succeeded Burnside as commander of the Army of the Potomac.*

**Above:** *A well equipped company of Federal troops, Company H of the 36th Pennsylvania Infantry.*

**Right:** *The 7th New York Cavalry encamped near Washington DC.*

troops, and drilled them incessantly. The intelligence service was reorganized, with the result that there were fewer of the exaggerated estimates of Lee's strength that had plagued McClellan. The pride and morale of the army rose with its physical condition and its numbers: by April there were 122,000 men in the infantry, 12,000 men in a well-trained cavalry, and 400 cannons. Hooker called it the greatest army on the planet and crowed, "May God have mercy on General Lee, for I will have none!"

In April, Lee's Army of Northern Virginia still lay along the Rappahannock at Fredericksburg. To dislodge them, Hooker devised a plan that was sound and imaginative: leaving a force to hold Lee in position, Hooker would march the bulk of his infantry around Fredericksburg in a wide strategic envelopment, crossing the river and coming in behind Lee from the west. In theory, the Confederates then had the choice of sitting and being destroyed or retreating and thus exposing their flank to the Federals.

**Opposite:** *Jeb Stuart's cavalry gave Lee a reconnaissance advantage at Chancellorsville.*

**Right:** *The Army of the Potomac marching in force along the Rappahannock on the way to Chancellorsville.*

**Below:** *Hooker's troops camped between rows of breastworks in the Wilderness.*

Hooker was sure his revitalized cavalry could take on Jeb Stuart now. Thus he prepared his campaign by sending 12,000 horsemen on a raid to cut Southern supply lines in the rear. Leaving on 13 April, the Union riders soon ran into floods on the rivers that held them up for two weeks, after which they ranged around to little purpose. Lee sent Stuart and his scouts to investigate this floundering maneuver, and after receiving the report simply ignored the Federal cavalry.

On 27 April Hooker struck camp, leaving 40,000 men under General John Sedgwick to hold Lee in place at Fredericksburg, and moved the rest of his army northwest and then south across fords on the Rappahannock and Rapidan. By 30 April these forces were gathered around Chancellorsville, which was simply a wide clearing with a mansion near to a road crossing. Surrounding the clearing was the virtually impenetrable forest of the Virginia Wilderness. On the 30th the Federals began marching towards Fredericksburg, ready to take the Rebels by surprise.

However, Robert E Lee had no intention of playing his assigned role in Hooker's little game. Lee and his generals had divined what Joe Hooker was going to do almost as soon as Hooker did. A Federal general recounts the information he found in a captured officer's diary:

> In March a council of war had been held at General Stuart's headquarters, which had been attended by Generals Jackson, A P Hill, Ewell, and Stuart. They were in conference over five hours, and came to the decision that the next battle would be at or near Chancellorsville, and that the position must be prepared.

On 30 April Jeb Stuart notified Lee that Hooker was moving his army from Chancellorsville toward the Confederate rear. At that time Lee had available some 60,000 men, less than half his enemy's strength (Longstreet and Hood had gone foraging in Virginia with a large detachment). Nonetheless, Lee once again boldly split his army to meet the Federal threat. A screen force of 10,000 men under General Jubal Early was left to hold Sedgwick at Fredericksburg and was ordered to build many fires to fool the Yankees. Lee and Stonewall Jackson marched northwest on 1 May to deal with Hooker's main body.

Hooker had seen the necessity of pushing past the dense woods of the Wilderness to meet Lee on open ground, where superior Federal artillery could have room to function and the army room to maneuver. On May Day morning the Federals pulled into open country, exactly where Hooker wanted to meet the enemy. Everything was going according to Hooker's plan; Fredericksburg lay less than a dozen miles away. Then, on high ground some two miles from Chancellorsville, around ten-thirty in the morning, Federal skirmishers ran into a line of Confederate skirmishers from Anderson's and McLaws' forces. As one Union soldier recalled, "There they stood facing each other, steady and silent, gazing, the one in apparent wonderment, the other in real surprise at the unexpected situation." Soon Federal units began moving up and easily forced the Rebel skirmishers back. All that seemed necessary for the North was to form line of battle and sweep the Rebels back toward Fredericksburg.

For every Federal general confronting Robert E Lee, there came a moment of truth: when the full realization of just how

dangerous Lee was, combined with the awful responsibility of holding in his hands the future of the American nation, came down on the Union commanding officer with the force of doom itself. On 1 May, with the Wilderness at his back and commanding vastly superior forces, Hooker began to act like a beaten man at the first brush with Lee that had not been part of his pretty plan. After several hours of inactivity he fled back to the reassuring safety of the forest, overruling the furious protests of his staff and ordering all his forces back towards Chancellorsville to dig into the Wilderness. The significance of this retreat was not lost on the Union troops.

During the afternoon of 1 May Jeb Stuart's cavalry had moved freely around the Union army, and late in the day Stuart reported to Lee that the Federal right was vulnerable, "in the air," with no real protection on the flank. A Confederate officer, Robert's nephew "Fitz" Lee, recalled Lee's response:

On May 1 General Lee wished to cut Hooker off from the United States Ford, preventing his communication with Sedgwick, and rode down himself and examined the lands all the way to the river, but found no place where he could execute this movement. Returning at night, he found Jackson and asked him if he knew of any place to attack. Jackson said he had been inquiring about roads and soon returned with the Reverend Doctor B T Lacey, who said a circuit could be made around by the Wilderness Tavern. A young man living in the country, and then in the cavalry, was sent for to act as guide. Lee and Jackson took their seats on a log to the north side of the Plank Road and a little distant from the wood. "General," Lee said, "we must get ready to attack the enemy, and you must make arrangements to move around his right flank."

The Confederates slept on the field that night. Waking in the early morning, one of Lee's staff saw an historic meeting: Jackson and Lee, finalizing their plans for yet another un-

**Above:** *At Chancellorsville on 3 May 1863 Hooker's Union Army briefly stems a Rebel breakthrough.*

**Opposite:** *The last meeting of Robert E Lee with Stonewall Jackson at Chancellorsville.*

pleasant surprise for Joe Hooker. It was to fall on that luckless Union right flank, O O Howard's XI Corps. Lee would divide forces again, holding Hooker's line of some 80,000 men in place with only 12,900 Confederates while Jackson marched 30,000 around to the west to strike the exposed Federal flank.

On the morning of 2 May 1863 the Union army was well fortified and easily handled probing attacks by the Rebels. The Federals little expected that these were feints to hold them in place; still less did they realize how thin Lee's line was in their front. Meanwhile, Jackson pulled his detachment out for the march across the front of the Union army, protected by the screen of the thick woods.

The XI Corps on the Union right was ill prepared to receive Jackson, though there had actually been fair warning of his maneuver. About noon Union general Dan Sickles had noticed Jackson's force moving to his right beyond the thick woods. Hooker, wondering at first if they were in fact headed for his right flank sent a cautionary note to Howard. But then Hooker began to convince himself that Lee must be retreating; in response to all further questions Hooker spent the afternoon insisting that the Rebels were hightailing it. When Sickles asked permission to move against the enemy column in his front, Hooker agreed, apparently figuring it would hasten the enemy in their retreat. Sickles cut his way through the brush with great difficulty and made contact with the end of the Confederate column. During the ensuing skirmish he captured some 500 men of a Georgia regiment. As these prisoners were being led to the rear, some were heard to jeer the Yanks. "You'll catch hell before night," and, "You wait until Jackson gets around to your right." (By then Jackson's column had apparently divined what their secretive commander was up to.) The Federals ignored these threats.

**Left:** *Stonewall Jackson's troops rout General Oliver O Howard's XI Corps.*

**Below:** *Generals Lee and Jackson conferring on the eye of the Battle of Chancellorsville.*

Meanwhile Hooker stripped his right flank of Barlow's division and sent them to help Sickles pursue the supposedly retreating rebels. As Sickles pulled away he left the rest of the XI Corps isolated and even more vulnerable than before.

At six o'clock in the afternoon the advance positions of the XI Corps were startled to see a mass of rabbits and deer scampering out of the woods towards them. The men whooped and laughed as the animals bolted towards the rear. There were scattered shots, and cannon suddenly appeared on the front. And then arose from thousands of throats the bone-chilling screech of the Rebel yell, and 26,000 of Stonewall Jackson's men came crashing through the Federal flank in a front a mile wide and four divisions deep, all of them shooting and screaming like demons.

Jackson's men moved straight down the enemy trenches, the 9000 men on the XI Corps fleeing in panic before them. Amidst the rout was General O O Howard, "in the middle of the roads and mounted, his maimed arm embracing a stand of colors . . . while with his sound arm he was gesticulating to the men to make a stand by their flag. With bared head he was pleading with his soldiers, literally weeping as he entreated the unheeding horde." Hooker knew nothing of the rout until he heard an aide screaming, "My God here they come!" A Union colonel remembered the appearance of the panic-stricken mob at Chancellorsville and the successful rally that followed:

It was a complete Bull Run rout. Men, horses, mules, rebel prisoners, wagons, guns, etc. etc. were coming down the road in terrible confusion, behind them an unceasing roar or musketry. We rode until we got into a mighty hot fire, and found that no one was attempting to make a stand, but every one running for his life. . . .

I found General Hooker sitting alone on his horse in front of the Chancellor House, and delivered my message; he merely said, "Very good, sir." I rode back and found the Eleventh Corps still surging up the road and still this terrible roar behind them. The rebels had received no check, but now troops began to march out on the plank road and form across it.

These troops were a division of the I Corps, whom Hooker had led forward and ordered, "Receive 'em on your bayo-

nets!" This infantry and the XII Corps artillery shoved through the fleeing men and hit the charging Rebels obliquely, slowing their advance on the left and center. Seeing a stand of Union artillery was in danger of being overrun on the right, General Alfred Pleasonton ordered Major Peter Keenan to charge his 8th Pennsylvania Cavalry into the Rebels, to buy time to turn the guns around. Keenan cheerfully accepted the order hardly knowing it was virtually suicidal. The cavalrymen, many of them scraped up from a poker game with no idea what was happening, rode directly into the middle of the oncoming enemy.

Though scores of Union saddles were emptied, the cavalry charge gave Pleasonton time to get 22 pieces aimed into the Rebels, and eventually the Federals had 36 more guns pelting the enemy from Fairview Cemetary. The Rebel advance halted before the cannonade, the troops becoming disorganized in the growing dark. Over in Hazel Grove, the 15,000 men of Sickles's III Corps had been cut off by Jackson's charge, and as night fell they began fighting their way back to

**Left:** *Panicked men of the Union XI Corps retreat before the onrushing Stonewall Brigade.*

**Below:** *Perched high in a tree, a Confederate sharpshooter takes careful aim.*

**Overleaf:** *Depiction of the fighting on 2 May and the wounding of Stonewall Jackson.*

their lines. After a hot and confused struggle in the gloom, with men falling from their own side's fire, part of the III Corps made it back while the rest settled into an uneasy bivouac in Hazel Grove.

Then at nine o'clock, amid the confusion of nighttime action, came the accident that was to temper this, Lee's greatest victory, with the most irreplaceable loss he had ever sustained. Stonewall Jackson had ridden out scouting from his lines just west of Chancellorsville. An officer of his staff recalled the tragedy that resulted:

From the order Jackson sent to General Stuart it was evident that his intention was to storm the enemy's works as soon as the lines were formed. While these orders were issued, Jackson started slowly along the pike toward the enemy. When we had ridden only a few rods, our little party was fired upon [by a group of Union infantry], the balls passing diagonally across the pike. . . . At the firing our horses wheeled suddenly to the left, and General Jackson galloped away into the woods to get out of range of the bullets, but had not gone over twenty steps ere the brigade to the left of the turnpike fired a volley. It was by this fire that Jackson was wounded [by three bullets, the most serious in the left arm]. We could distinctly hear General Hill calling, at the top of his voice, to his troops to cease firing. I was alongside Jackson and saw his arm fall at his side, loosing the rein. The limb of a tree took off his cap and threw him flat on the back of his horse. I rode after him, but Jackson soon regained his seat, caught the bridle in his right hand, and turning his horse toward our men, somewhat checked his speed. I caught his horse as he reached the pike. . . .

I dismounted, and seeing that he was faint, I asked the General what I could do for him, or if he felt able to ride as far as into our lines. He answered, "You had best take me down," leaning as he spoke toward me and then falling, partially fainting from loss of blood. I caught him in my arms and held him until Captain Wynn could get his feet out of the stirrups, then we carried him a few steps and laid him on the ground.

Jackson was placed on a litter, and with his bearers came under heavy artillery fire before they could reach an ambulance. That night Jackson's left arm was amputated and he began slowly to sink. Hearing the news that Jackson had been wounded by his own troops, Lee responded prophetically, "Jackson has lost his left arm but I have lost my right arm."

Also during the night, Federals bivouacking near Chancellorsville heard a strange, muffled firing. It was soon discovered, to the men's horror, that the Wilderness was burning and the woods were full of wounded; the sound was that of of exploding muskets and cartridge cases. Soldiers dashed into the woods and removed the few wounded they could reach. And then the survivors sat and listened: "Curses and yells of pain, piteous appeals and spasmodic prayers could be distinguished ... the flames roared more fiercely, the cries grew fainter, until at last they were hushed."

Taking over Jackson's corps, Jeb Stuart rallied the men with the name of their stricken leader and led a savage attack at five in the morning of 3 May. Stuart caught the Federal III Corps in motion back toward their lines and pushed them out of high ground at Hazel Grove, whence 30 Rebel cannons were brought to bear on the heart of the Federal position at Chancellorsville. The clearing around Hooker's headquarters quickly became a maelstrom of shot and shell. Then the Rebels began shoving the Federals back toward the Rappahannock River.

That morning, 3 May, as the Confederate attack was tearing into the Union lines, Sedgwick mounted a series of assaults on Jubal Early's men outside Fredericksburg at Marye's Heights, where Burnside had been so tragically repulsed in December, and finally stormed the position with heavy losses by eleven in the morning. Sedgwick then moved toward Chancellorsville, hoping to catch Lee in a vise.

On the front porch of the Chancellor mansion, his headquarters, General Hooker seemed paralyzed amidst the furious enemy fire that was destroying his batteries one by one, smashing into the house, exploding in the upper rooms and sending showers of brick fragments flying in every direction. As he stood on the front porch leaning on a pillar, straining for the sound of Sedgwick's approach, Hooker was thrown to the ground by a shell that splintered the pillar. Dazed, he gave Couch temporary command and ordered a withdrawal to entrenchments already prepared in an arc between the Rapidan and Rappahannock. The Rebels pursued this withdrawal, their cannons firing everything they could lay their hands on – including old railroad iron, chains and tools. The woods burned again, consuming the dead and wounded of both sides.

Then Lee put the finishing touch on his masterpiece. Leaving Stuart with 25,000 men to hold Hooker's dug-in 80,000,

Lee marched with 20,000 men to confront Sedgwick's advance on his rear. Sedgwick ran into General Lafayette McLaws's troops around Salem Church on that afternoon of 3 May. By next morning Lee had surrounded Sedgwick on three sides with McLaws, R H Anderson, and Early, while also re-occupying Marye's Heights with William Barksdale's men. Sedgwick was driven back to Bank's Ford on the Rappahannock, where the Rebels harassed him strongly. The Federal division withdrew across the ford on the night of 4 May.

Lee began planning an all-out offensive against Hooker's remaining division for 6 May, an offensive that might well have been a disaster for the South given the strength of the Federal entrenchments. Concerning this plan, Confederate

General Edward P Alexander circumspectly but wryly commented, "It must be conceded that Lee never in his life took a more audacious resolve than when he determined to assault Hooker's entrenchments."

But Hooker had already had enough. Over the objections of most of his staff he withdrew across the Rappahannock during the miserably wet and muddy night of 5 May. He had gone into battle with a better than two to one advantage and had nonetheless let his forces be outnumbered in every encounter; indeed, some 30,000 Union troops had never been committed at all.

Years later, Hooker was to make a simple confession about himself at Chancellorsville, when he confronted the battlefield genius of Lee and his army: "To tell the truth, I just lost confidence in Joe Hooker."

In contrast, the morale of the Army of Northern Virginia was never so exultant, their confidence in themselves and their leaders never more unshakable. But such confidence is dangerous in armies and in leaders, as the Army of Northern Virginia was about to learn. And glorious as Lee's victory at Chancellorsville was, it was a Pyrrhic one. Casualty figures are uncertain; Lee had about 12,821 in killed, missing and wounded to Union's 17,278. But while the Federals had lost 13 percent of their army, Lee had lost 22 percent of his. Numbers were beginning to count in the war; the South's supply of manpower was limited and becoming more critical with every battle won or lost.

On 10 May Stonewall Jackson cried out in delirium from his bed, "Order A P Hill to prepare for action – pass the infantry to the front rapidly – tell Major Hawks . . ." And then, after a silence, "No, let us cross over the river and rest under the shade of the trees." On that enigmatic word of peace the great warrior died.

**Left:** *Southern artillery: crucial to the victory at Chancellorsville.*

**Below:** *Stonewall Jackson's death from wounds on 10 May saddened the South.*

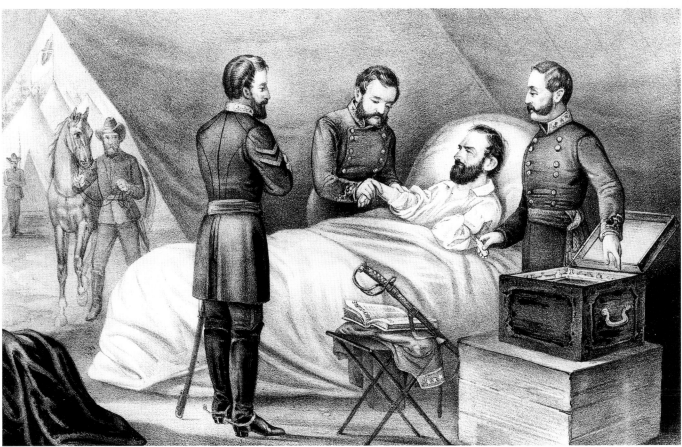

# CHICKAMAUGA

As he had done in 1862 after his victory at Second Manassas, Lee proposed to follow up his triumph at Chancellorsville with a second invasion of the North. This time his target was different – Pennsylvania rather than Maryland – and his army was considerably larger and stronger than before, but the strategic considerations that suggested this move were less sanguine than those of 1862. Although the war had so far been going well for the Confederacy in the East, it was going badly in the West: the Mississippi was all but lost, and once Union General Ulysses S Grant succeeded in capturing Vicksburg, he would be free to turn his full attention on Tennessee, perhaps slashing across that state, bursting into Georgia and cutting the South in half. At the same time, the Confederacy was also not faring well on the home front. All Southern hope of foreign recognition was now dead, and the Union's ever-tightening blockade was causing mounting public privation and financial chaos.

Thus Lee's proposed second invasion of the North was as much a product of desperation as of optimism. What Lee wanted was one final, truly decisive victory in the East, one that would either win the war at a stroke or at least be so crushing as to leave his armies free to deal with the threat from the West. Some other Southern commanders, notably Longstreet, disagreed, arguing that the time to deal with the Western problem was now, and that any offensive actions that might be taken by the Union Army of the Potomac in the interim could probably be frustrated by relatively light defending forces in Virginia. How much merit Longstreet's view had is impossible to say, for it was Lee's strategy that was adopted.

The result of this great gamble was the Civil War's most famous battle and the South's most shocking defeat. In the first three days of July 1863, on and around the low hills that lie just south of the small town of Gettysburg, Pennsylvania, Lee lost a third of his army – 28,063 killed, wounded or missing. The North had not fared much better – 23,049 total casualties – but the crucial difference was that the Union could make good such losses and the Confederacy now could not. After the catastrophe of Gettysburg the South would be incapable of mounting any more important offensive operations in the Eastern Theater.

And there was good reason to suppose that the same would be true of the Western Theater as well. So far, the South had lost every major engagement fought deep within

**Opposite:** *Dead soldiers on the field after Gettysburg, the South's most shocking defeat.*

**Right:** *By the end of the third day of fighting Gettysburg was the war's costliest battle.*

**Below:** *Southerners attempt to breach the Union defenses at Cemetery Hill during the Battle of Gettysburg.*

its own territory, and most of these defeats had been at the hands of the tight-lipped, hard-fighting Ulysses S Grant. In a string of brilliant victories rivalling Lee's, Grant had risen from utter obscurity to fame with his operations at Shiloh, Forts Henry Dead Donelson, and, most of all, in the year-long campaign, extraordinary for its boldness and innovation, around the vital Mississippi River city of Vicksburg, which fell to the Union the same day as the Battle of Gettysburg concluded, 3 July 1863.

Those two Northern victories, Gettysburg and Vicksburg, were the decisive ones of the conflict, when the fortunes of war turned the corner that would lead inexorably to victory for the North. Ironically, the decisive year of 1863 had been was ushered in by the indecisive battle of Stone's River, near Murfreesboro, Tennessee. There, in three days of fighting between the Federal Army of the Cumberland and the Confederate Army of Tennessee, 20,000 men had fallen to no advantage to either side. For nearly six months thereafter

**Above:** *General Braxton Bragg commanded the Confederate Army of Tennessee at the Battle of Chickamauga.*

those two armies sat some 40 miles apart, waiting for their next great confrontation.

Commanding the Southern forces was General Braxton Bragg, a veteran of the Mexican War and a trusted friend of President Jefferson Davis. That friendship was not to bode well for the Confederacy. Bragg was an intelligent man but a poor leader, a great maker of plans who could not bring them to fruition.

Bragg's Federal counterpart, General William S Rosecrans, had earned his command by demonstrating a considerable talent for strategy. Early in the war Rosecrans had driven the Confederates from West Virginia, and later and been of great service to Grant in Mississippi. Rosecrans was meticulous in planning campaigns down to the last wagonwheel; he was also maddeningly slow to move. After the standoff at Stone's River, the obvious goal of his Army of the Cumberland was what was perhaps the last remaining truly vital city of the Confederacy – Chattanooga.

The city lay in the southeastern corner of Tennessee, near

**Right:** *The city of Chattanooga in wartime. It was an important strategic center for the South.*

the corners of Alabama and Georgia on the banks of the Tennessee River. Railroads converged on it from all over the South. For the Confederacy, Chattanooga was the best base for operations in Tennessee and Kentucky; for the North, it was the gateway to Atlanta and all of Georgia. For these reasons, Chattanooga was the real strategic center of the Confederacy. If it were to be conquered by the Union, much of the Southern war effort would be hamstrung.

In the first six months of 1863 Bragg's Confederate Army of Tennessee lay in Tullahoma, on the road between Rosecrans's army (near Murfreesboro) and Chattanooga. In May the Federal high command began to pressure Rosecrans to move against Bragg; this would not only threaten Chattanooga but would keep Bragg from sending men to reinforce Vicksburg, which was now besieged by Grant. Rosecrans waffled and Bragg did send some troops to Mississippi.

In mid-June Rosecrans finally got his army moving and at once demonstrated his strategic skills. He threatened the Rebel left flank with cavalry, and when Bragg attempted to meet this threat he discovered that two Union corps, those of George H Thomas and Thomas L Crittenden, had gotten behind the Confederate right. Confused and helpless, Bragg was forced after 30 June to pull back to his nearest stronghold – Chattanooga.

Rosecrans had made a brilliant tactical move, but then he stopped again, asking for reinforcements. These were soon available, after the fall of Vicksburg in early July. But then Washington decided to occupy conquered territory rather than reinforce Rosecrans. Meanwhile, Bragg was heavily reinforced, most notably in mid-July by General Daniel H Hill, formerly of Lee's army. Also on the way were two divisions under Longstreet, which were now available after Gettysburg. (Longstreet had suggested a move much like this well before Gettysburg).

On 5 August Rosecrans was imperatively ordered to move against Bragg. Now he faced the problem of getting the Confederates out of heavily-fortified Chattanooga. Bragg had reorganized his army to defend the city – there were two divi-

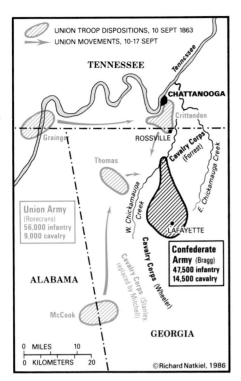

UNION TROOP DISPOSITIONS, 10 SEPT 1863
UNION MOVEMENTS, 10-17 SEPT

TENNESSEE

CHATTANOOGA

Crittenden

ROSSVILLE

Grainger

Thomas

Cavalry Corps (Forrest)

W. Chickamauga Creek

E. Chickamauga Creek

Union Army
(Rosecrans)
56,000 infantry
9,000 cavalry

ALABAMA

LAFAYETTE

Cavalry Corps (Wheeler)
replaced by Mitchell)

Cavalry Corps (Stanley, replaced by Mitchell)

McCook

Confederate
Army (Bragg)
47,500 infantry
14,500 cavalry

GEORGIA

0   MILES        10
0   KILOMETERS       20

©Richard Natkiel, 1986

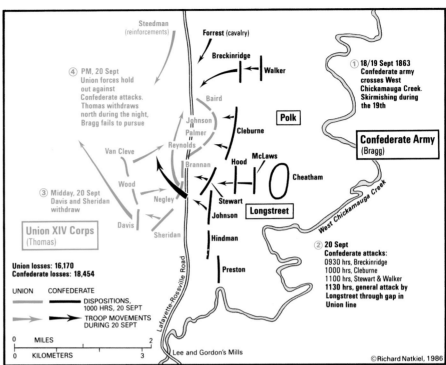

Steedman
(reinforcements)

Forrest (cavalry)

Breckinridge    Walker

④ PM, 20 Sept
Union forces hold
out against
Confederate attacks.
Thomas withdraws
north during the night,
Bragg fails to pursue

Baird

Johnson
Palmer            Cleburne

Polk

Van Cleve

Reynolds

① 18/19 Sept 1863
Confederate army
crosses West
Chickamauga Creek.
Skirmishing during
the 19th

Confederate Army
(Bragg)

Brannan      Hood   McLaws

Wood                               Cheatham

③ Midday, 20 Sept
Davis and Sheridan
withdraw

Negley          Stewart

Union XIV Corps
(Thomas)

Johnson    Longstreet

Davis

Sheridan

Hindman

West Chickamauga Creek

Union losses: 16,170
Confederate losses: 18,454

Preston

UNION    CONFEDERATE

② 20 Sept
Confederate attacks:
0930 hrs, Breckinridge
1000 hrs, Cleburne
1100 hrs, Stewart & Walker
1130 hrs, general attack by
Longstreet through gap in
Union line

DISPOSITIONS,
1000 HRS, 20 SEPT

TROOP MOVEMENTS
DURING 20 SEPT

0   MILES        2
0   KILOMETERS       3

Lafayette-Rossville Road

Lee and Gordon's Mills

©Richard Natkiel, 1986

**Above:** *Operations in the Western Theater during September 1863.*

**Below:** *Union commander William S Rosecrans was a careful strategist but slow to move.*

**Right:** *General George Thomas (left), afterward known as the "Rock of Chickamauga," held against the Southern attack and prevented a Union rout.*

**Below:** *Confederate troops charge a Union line.*

sions each under Leonidas Polk, D H Hill, Simon B Buckner and W H T Walker, with cavalry under Joseph Wheeler and the brilliant Nathan Bedford Forrest (though Forrest only worked well in independent commands).

Rosecrans tried another strategic gambit, and it worked handsomely, abetted by Bragg's poor intelligence-gathering: Federal columns appeared along the Tennessee River at several widely-spaced points; as Bragg hesitated, worrying about his supply line to the rear, the Federal army crossed the river unopposed west of the city and Crittenden marched on Chattanooga.

Confronted by an enemy seeming to appear all over the map, Bragg evacuated Chattanooga on 6 September and headed south into Georgia. It was actually a wise move on Bragg's part – he was getting out of town with his army while the getting was good. Certain that they had the enemy forces on the run, the Federals made haste to pursue them into Georgia. Rosecrans boasted he would chase the Rebels to Atlanta, if not clear to the sea.

But in fact, Rosecrans was marching his army into a trap. Bragg was not fleeing; instead, he was concentrating his forces near Lafayette, Georgia, and preparing to turn and destroy the Federal army. Whether Bragg had actually planned the trap in advance is debatable. D H Hill later wrote about Bragg at that time, "The truth is, General Bragg was bewildered by 'the popping out of the rats from so many holes.' The wide dispersion of the Federal forces, and their confronting him at so many points, perplexed him, instead of being a source of congratulation that such grand opportunities were offered for crushing them one by one."

The wide dispersion Hill mentions refers to Rosecrans's deployments as he moved into Georgia – the three Union corps were spread out over 50 miles of rugged country, moving through three narrow gaps in the long ridge called Lookout Mountain. Bragg had merely to bring his superior numbers to bear and crush them in detail, one corps at a time. The Federal army was ripe for the picking.

Deliberate trap or not, Bragg and his generals proceeded to spring it ineptly. The forces of General Leonidas Polk were ordered to attack Thomas on 10 September. Though Polk's men appeared in Thomas's path, nothing happened. Another attack failed to materialize on the 11th. Two days later Bragg

arrived at Chickamauga Creek, expecting Polk to have anni-
hilated Crittenden's corps there. Polk had not budged.

The continuing presence of parties of Confederates in his
front, all of whom seemed to be withdrawing towards
Lafayette, finally tipped off Rosecrans that he was in serious
trouble. On 12 September he urgently ordered his wings to
converge toward the center and concentrate on the west side
of Chickamauga Creek, near Lafayette. Bragg, meanwhile,
was also concentrating his forces near the creek and was im-
patiently awaiting the arrival of Longstreet's divisions. When
they arrived Bragg would have over 65,000 men to Rosecrans's less than 60,000.

Rosecrans had divined what Bragg's strategy would be in
the battle, which was to move around the Union left and cut
off their line of retreat – road to Chattanooga. The Federal
commander thus paid special attention to his left, placing
General George H Thomas in command there. The posi-
tioning of the indomitable Thomas was to prove a decision
most fortunate indeed for the fate of the Union army.

On the night of the 18th both sides prepared for battle,
Rosecrans building a strong defensive position. Because of
the thick woods in the area, neither general knew where his
enemy was – or, indeed, where his own forces were. Bragg
thought the Union left was at Lee's and Gordon's Mill, and
planned his attack to flank that position and gain the road to
Chattanooga. Since Rosecrans had anticipated that, he had
strung his lines out north from the mill and along the road. By
daybreak on 19 September Thomas had formed his line of
battle above the steep sides of Horseshoe Ridge.

As dawn came on the 19th, both armies were poised for
battle at Chickamauga Creek. Prophetically, the creek's name

came from an old Cherokee Indian word meaning "River of
Death."

The battle began by accident. Unsure whether there were
Confederates north of the creek, Thomas sent cavalry to
scout his front. Soon these men stumbled on some of Forrest's cavalrymen, who were dismounted on the Reed's
Bridge road. The Southerners retreated under fire back to
their infantry, who then pushed forward. Slowly the battle
spread outward until both armies were firing all along the
line. There followed a confused but nonetheless bloody day
of fighting. As Hill later wrote, "it was the sparring of the
amateur boxer, and not the crushing blows of the trained
pugilist." All morning there was a gap of some two miles in
the Federal lines, but it was hours before Bragg found the gap
and tried to exploit. Finally, an attempt was made by the
forces of John B Hood, whose division of Longstreet's command had just arrived ahead of the others. Hood smashed the
right center of the Union line and got on to the Chattanooga
road, but a wave of Federals charged in to drive them back.

After a day of heavy but indecisive fighting on 19 September the guns fell silent in the late afternoon. By then Longstreet had arrived by rail with the rest of his forces. It took
him until eleven at night to find Bragg, who got out of bed for
a conference. Dividing his army into two wings, Bragg gave
the right to Polk and the left to Longstreet. Polk was to begin
at dawn with a strong assault on Thomas; after Polk's attack
there were to be successive attacks down the line to the
south. As the Confederate general spoke they heard the
sound of axes from the Federal lines – the Army of the Cumberland was building a strong defensive line of log breastworks through the thick woods.

At dawn on the 20th visibility was negligible due to the woods and a thick blanket of fog. Bragg sat in his head-quarters straining to hear the sound of Polk's dawn attack. After an hour of inactivity a messenger was dispatched to find Polk. The general was discovered reading a newspaper on a farmhouse porch while waiting for his breakfast. When queried about his attack, Polk grandly responded, "Do tell General Bragg that my heart is overflowing with anxiety for the attack – overflowing with anxiety, sir!" When this was reported at about nine-thirty to Bragg, he swore, "in a manner that would have powerfully assisted a mule team in getting up a mountain," and ordered Polk to begin the attack on Thomas immediately.

By this time the front stretched some two miles, north to south, Polk's men fell with a will onto Thomas, who held on to his breastworks in the Horseshoe Ridge but soon found his more vulnerable left flank being pushed across the vital road to Chattanooga. Again and again Thomas called for re-inforcements from Rosecrans, to whom he had a direct tele-graph wire (one of the first of these on any battlefield). Con-fusion began to creep into Union deployments due to the thick woods. At eleven in the morning this confusion created a strange and catastrophic turn in the battle. An aide, who had been riding behind the Union position, reported to Rose-crans that there was a gap in the Federal line between T J Wood's and J J Reynolds's divisions. Intending to seal that gap, Rosecrans hurriedly sent an order to Wood to move left, to "close up on and support" Reynolds (both these divisions lay near the Federal right flank, which was so far inactive).

But the aide had made a disastrous mistake: there was no gap in the Union line. Between Wood and Reynolds was John Brannan's division, exactly where they were supposed to be, but so hidden by the woods that the aide had not seen them.

Wood received Rosecrans's order and puzzled over it. How was he to "close up on and support" Reynolds when Brannan

was between them? Finally Wood decided that "support" was the operative idea and ordered his division to pull out of line and march behind Brannan towards Reynolds. His men formed line of march and headed for the rear, leaving a gap-ing hole in the Union right wing.

At just that moment, hardly a stone's throw away but still hidden in the woods, Longstreet was massing eight brigades for the attack. (That the attack was gathering then and there was apparently sheer coincidence.) At the head of the column rode hard-fighting John B Hood. About eleven-thirty

**Opposite:** *A Rebel attempt to take a Union battery at Chickamauga is foiled by Lieutenant Van Pelt and his men.*

**Right:** *Confederate General John Bell Hood.*

**Below:** *Southern marksmen in the Chickamauga woods.*

in the morning the Confederates headed for the Union lines and found to their astonishment that no one was there.

The results were immediate and dramatic. A solid column of screaming Rebels flooded straight through the Union line, crashed on to the end of Wood's departing column, and scatted the divisions of Federal generals Philip Sheridan and Jefferson C Davis, who had begun moving into the gap from the right. Hood, having lost the use of an arm at Gettysburg, was wounded seriously in the leg, but his men pushed on.

During this rout the Federals lost thousands in casualties and captured; Hill later wrote that he had never seen Federal dead so thickly blanketing the ground except after the suicidal charge at Fredericksburg. Among the fleeing were a panicky and demoralized Rosecrans and most of his staff. Assuming his whole army was routed, Rosecrans ordered everyone to retreat to Chattanooga.

Fortunately for the Union, not everyone obeyed that order, because Rosecrans was wrong about his forces being totally beaten. Along Horseshoe Ridge, to the left, Thomas was holding on like grim death, with thousands of enemy swarming

**Left:** *The fight at Orchard Knob, one of a number of battles near Chattanooga in November 1863.*

**Above:** *Ulysses Grant, the new Union commander, views the fighting at Chattanooga.*

danger. Yet not all the routed Federal divisions had continued on to Chattanooga. Wood, Brannan and Reynolds fell into position on Thomas's right, Wood meeting the first appearance of Longstreet's men with a determined bayonet charge that stopped the Rebels in their tracks. As Thomas's line on the right stabilized a little, Rebel assaults swarmed on to his left flank. D H Hill later wrote admiringly of Thomas's stand, "that indomitable Virginia soldier, George H Thomas, was there and was destined to save the Union army from total rout and ruin, by confronting with invincible pluck the forces of his friend and captain [Bragg] in the Mexican War."

As the afternoon wore on Thomas's Federals were running out of ammunition, their front and flanks were staggering under heavy assaults, and the enemy was moving around the right flank to the rear. Rebel cannons were moving into position to enfilade the Union right, and there were no men left to do anything about it. And then, at three-thirty, Thomas noticed a column of dust approaching in his rear. If the troops that were making that dust were foe, his men were doomed. An officer was dispatched to take a look. They proved to be friends, part of two divisions of reserves commanded by General Gordon Granger, who had just committed a serious and most salutary breach of orders. Placed in reserve by Rosecrans, with strict orders to guard the road to Chattanooga, Granger had listened with increasing anxiety to the sound of battle growing steadily on the Federal left. Finally, he made his own decision – "I am going to Thomas, orders or no orders." By four o'clock Granger was shaking hands with an overjoyed Thomas, men and ammunition arriving rapidly behind them. Granger's men cleared the enemy from a valley in the rear, and a path of retreat was at last open.

The South had won the field at Chickamauga, one of the greatest victories of the war in the Western Theater. But General George Thomas had saved the Federal army to fight another day, becoming in the process one of the immortal heroes of the Union cause. To history, Thomas is forever "The Rock of Chickamauga."

Casualties in the battle were among the worst of the war: of 66,326 Southerners engaged, there were 2312 killed, 14,674 wounded, 1468 missing, a total of 18,454 casualties; for the North, of 58,222 engaged, there were 1657 killed, 9756 wounded, 4757 missing, a total of 16,170. Altogether, nearly 35,000 men fell; both sides had lost 28 percent of their forces.

Back in his headquarters, Bragg could not seem to get it

around the steep sides of the ridge. At Confederate headquarters Longstreet was begging General Bragg to give him all his remaining troops to surround Thomas's position. Bragg, seemingly of the opinion that his army was losing, replied that the rest of the men had "no fight left in them." Having fought at the side of Lee most of the war, Longstreet's frustration with the obtuse Bragg must have been titanic.

By mid-afternoon Thomas was watching enemy forces moving towards his right. He knew his front along the precipitous slopes was strong, but his flanks were in great

**Left:** *An N C Wyeth portrait of General Grant. His arrival at Chattanooga transformed an impending Union disaster into a successful offensive.*

**Opposite top:** *Confederate General John B Hood is wounded at Chickamauga. He lost his right leg.*

**Opposite bottom:** *General Thomas's men repel a Rebel charge at Chickamauga.*

into his head that he had won. His generals pressed him to pursue, the impetuous Forrest screaming at his commander, "You are a coward and a damned scoundrel!" By next morning, 21 September, Bragg was finally willing to admit victory. He sent a force to Missionary Ridge in Chattanooga with orders to attack; but Bragg's men found the Federals "ready to receive and entertain us."

Yet Bragg had one more chance to reclaim Chattanooga. He put his army in strong position on the ridges and settled in to starve the Yankees out. The Federal army was now besieged deep in enemy territory. And starve the Yankees did, while both Bragg and Rosecrans spent their time writing elaborate reports blaming their subordinates for everything.

On 23 October 1863 General Ulysses S Grant arrived in Chattanooga. He had been appointed to command of most Union forces west of the Alleghenies. His first act was to replace the spent Rosecrans with Thomas as commander of the Army of the Cumberland. Gaining reinforcements, Grant soon had food and supplies flowing into the city. And on 25

November the vindictive Federals, shouting "Chickamauga!" as they charged, swarmed up and over the slopes of Missionary Ridge and chased the Confederate Army of Tennessee back to Georgia in one of the worst routs the Confederacy ever suffered. Chattanooga, the strategic center of the South, was secure for the Union. Now the way was prepared for William Tecumseh Sherman's devastating march across Georgia to the sea.

Contemplating this last golden opportunity lost, General D H Hill later concluded:

It seems to me that the *élan* of the Southern soldier was never seen after Chickamauga – that brilliant dash which had distinguished him was gone forever. He was too intelligent not to know that the cutting in two of Georgia meant death to all his hopes . . . He fought stoutly to the last, but, after Chickamauga, with the sullenness of despair and without the enthusiasm of hope. That "barren victory" sealed the fate of the Southern Confederacy.

**W**hen, at the end of 1863, Ulysses S Grant lifted the siege of Chattanooga, the Union was at last in a position to begin its invasion of the Deep South. But the anticipated lunge into Georgia did not start immediately. Early in the new year Grant was recalled to Washington, where he was created lieutenant general (a rank held previously only by George Washington), placed in charge of all the Union armies and given the task of devising a strategy for winning the war. When it emerged, that strategy, in essence, involved not one invasion but two: the thrust into Georgia, to be commanded by Sherman, would be coordinated with a simultaneous drive south from Washington aimed at Richmond – this latter operation to be conducted by General George Meade under Grant's personal supervision.

Both offensives began on the night of 3-4 May 1864. Within two days, Grant's part of the operation had become embroiled in savage fighting with Lee's Army of Northern Virginia, and this continued almost unabated for the next six weeks. Time and again – in The Wilderness, at Spotsylvania, at North Anna and at Cold Harbor – Lee attempted to block Grant's advance, and each time, after a bloody confrontation, Grant would disengage, swing around to the east and continue his relentless drive southward. By 18 June Grant was actually south of Richmond, facing Lee's strongly fortified position at Petersburg. At this point Grant abandoned maneuver and settled in for a long siege, reasoning that since Petersburg was the most important rail junction supplying Richmond, it was as good a place as any to begin starving the Rebel capital into submission. It was also a good – perhaps necessary – place to pause and try to recover from the rigors of the campaign thus far. The casualties on both sides had been appalling: 50,000 (41 percent) for the Union and 32,000 (46 percent) for the Confederacy. Given Lee's lack of reserve manpower, the figures were more ominous for the South than even the numbers and percentages might suggest.

Meanwhile, Sherman, fighting all the way, slowly made his

**Above:** *Remains of a Confederate battle flag. Many Southern units refused to surrender their banners but burned, buried, or hid them.*

**Left:** *Richmond, burned by Rebel soldiers as they prepared to abandon the Southern capital.*

**Opposite:** *A Union mortar battery prepares its position. Such siege weapons represent the North's overwhelming military strength.*

way towards Atlanta. He invested the Georgia capital in July, finally captured it in September and, after burning much of it, left it on 15 November to begin his infamous march to Savannah and the sea. Leaving a 60-mile-wide swath of calculated destruction in his wake, he reached and took Savannah on 21 December. A few days earlier, Union General George Thomas, the "Rock of Chickamauga," had, on Sherman's orders, engaged and all but destroyed the army of Confederate General John Bell Hood in Tennessee. There was now hardly any major military organization left in the Confederacy that might be sent to reinforce Lee at Petersburg.

By early 1865 it was obvious to all that the end was near. Sherman had wheeled north into the Carolina, and there seemed little hope that a hastily-improvised Confederate force under Joseph E Johnston could long deter Sherman from his ultimate objective: junction with Grant outside Petersburg. There were no great battles left to the Confederacy now, only the slow agony of failing strength and hope in the trenches of Petersburg. On 2 April 1865, after six months of devastating siege, Lee and the remains of his army bolted from Petersburg. Lee was making a last desperate effort to join forces with Johnston's army in South Carolina, but his leaving doomed Richmond. Lee was run to ground by Grant and General Philip Sheridan, who circled and harried the pathetic remains of the Army of Northern Virginia until that 9 April at Appomattox when Lee's men made their last charge, breaking through the center of Sheridan's line as it blocked their path. For a brief moment there was open country in front of the Army of Northern Virginia. Then from over a hill appeared Union infantry, line after line of blue, marching to fill that last gateway to freedom. Soon from

within Confederate lines came a rider carrying a white flag into the ranks of the enemy.

The war was over. Lee's surrender to Grant at Appomattox on 9 April 1865 largely ended the hostilities (Johnston surrendered to Sherman on the 8th). Now the country was one again, the glorious exploits of the men in gray a matter of history and proud memory.

Throughout the long days of the war a volunteer nurse in Union military hospitals had put into impassioned words this thoughts about the struggle. He was Walt Whitman, later to be recognized as the great poet of the reborn nation. At the war's conclusion, Whitman wrote this benediction:

The dead in this war – there they lie, strewing the fields and woods and valleys and battlefields of the South: Virginia, the Peninsula, Malvern Hill and Fair Oaks, the banks of the Chickahominy, the terraces of Fredericksburg, Antietam bridge, the grisly ravines of Manassas, the bloody promenade of the Wilderness.

The dead, the dead, the dead . . . somewhere they crawled to die, alone, in bushes, low gullies, or on the sides of hills . . . Our young men once so handsome and so joyous, taken from us . . . the clusters of camp graves . . . the single graves left in the woods or by the roadside . . . the general million, and the special cemeteries in almost all the states.

The infinite dead, the land entire saturated, perfumed with their impalpable ashes' exhalation in Nature's chemistry distilled; and shall be so forever in every future grain of wheat and ear of corn, and every flower that grows, and every breath we draw.

**Opposite:** *A Union soldier surveys a ruined Richmond and its still-standing Southern capitol.*

**Right:** *Union soldiers at Appomattox Court House pose after the surrender ceremony.*

**Below:** *Grant and others (Sheridan between Grant and Lee, Meade at Grant's left) with General Lee at the McLean house at Appomattox Court House on 9 April 1865.*

# INDEX

*Page numbers in italics refer to illustrations*